SURGICAL SPEED
SHOOTING

HOW TO ACHIEVE HIGH-SPEED
MARKSMANSHIP IN A GUNFIGHT

Paladin Press
Boulder, Colorado

ANDY STANFORD

Other titles by Andy Stanford:

Advanced Fighting with Firearms (video)
Combat Rifle Marksmanship Training Exercises
Combat Riflecraft (video)
Fight at Night: Tools, Techniques, Tactics, and Training for Combat in Low-Light
  and Darkness
Fighting with Firearms (video)
Martial Marksmanship (video, with Michael D. Janich)

Surgical Speed Shooting:
How to Achieve High-Speed Marksmanship in a Gunfight
by Andy Stanford

Copyright © 2001 by Andy Stanford
ISBN 10: 1-58160-143-3
ISBN 13: 978-1-58160-143-5
Printed in the United States of America

Published by Paladin Press, a division of
Paladin Enterprises, Inc.
Gunbarrel Tech Center
7077 Winchester Circle
Boulder, Colorado 80301 USA
+1.303.443.7250

Direct inquiries and/or orders to the above address.

PALADIN, PALADIN PRESS, and the "horse head" design
are trademarks belonging to Paladin Enterprises and
registered in United States Patent and Trademark Office.

Visit our Web site at www.paladin-press.com

Cover photos of James Yeager (front) and Andy Stanford (back) by Don Reber.

Front cover: James Yeager demonstrates the modern isosceles.

CONTENTS

ACKNOWLEDGMENTS

This book would not have been possible without the contributions of my fellow isosceles-preaching instructors Massad Ayoob (Lethal Force Institute), Bill Rogers (Institute of Advanced Weaponcraft), Ron Avery (The Practical Shooting Academy), Frank Garcia (Universal Shooting Academy), Greg Hamilton (Insights Training Center), John Holschen (Insights Training Center), Dave Vaughan (Urban Firearms Institute), John Shaw (Mid-South Institute), Ross Sanders (Mid-South Institute), Jim "Doc" Montgomery (Mid-South Institute), Lou Chiodo (California Highway Patrol), Mike Janich (Paladin Press), Jim Cirillo, and the late, great Col. Rex Applegate.

I have also incorporated ideas on combat marksmanship technique from Rob Leatham, Matt Burkett, Jerry Miculek (secondhand), "Jim Grover" (via videocassette), Jerry Barnhart (likewise), Brian Enos (via his book), and J. Michael Plaxco (ditto).

The gun-handling chapters additionally reflect the efforts of Jeff Cooper (American Pistol Institute), Bill Jeans (API), Michael Harries (API), Michael Horne (API), Louis Awerbuck (Yavapai Firearms Academy), Randy Cain (Cumberland Tactics), Clint Smith (Thunder Ranch), Bert DuVernay (S&W Academy), Jim Crews (Marksman's Enterprise), Tom Givens (Range Master), George Harris (SigArms Academy) Jim Higginbotham (Range Master), Dane Burns (Range Master), John Farnam (Defense Training International), Gabe Suarez (Suarez International), Chuck Taylor (ASAA), Max Joseph (Tactical Firearms Training Team), John Meyer (Heckler & Koch), and Lyle Wyatt (W&W, now OPS SoCal).

Special thanks to fellow IDPA Master Steve Moses (OPS Southwest), Tony Torre (OPS Miami), Dr. David L.G. Arnold (U.S. Military Academy, West Point), and Irv Lehman for reviewing my draft.

And last but not least, Jon Ford and the good folks at Paladin Press, a supportive and ethical company.

FOREWORD
by James Yeager

As a tactical team leader, the biggest compliment I can pay any man is to have him back me up while serving high-risk warrants. Andy Stanford has earned that respect. He served as my personal cover officer during joint operations conducted by our department (Big Sandy, Tennessee, PD), other local agencies, the 24th Judicial District Drug Task Force, the Tennessee Bureau of Investigation, and the Drug Enforcement Administration. Make no mistake: Andy is a man who can handle himself in serious situations. He is someone who can be relied upon, and he can go through a door with me anytime.

Anyone even remotely familiar with contemporary combat firearms training knows Andy as a nationally acclaimed instructor, author, and, perhaps more importantly, advocate of sound tactics and the combat mind-set. He reached this status through more than two decades of dedicated training and study. Listing his extensive resumé would take several pages. A Master Class IDPA shooter and National Tactical Invitational "Shotist" (1st overall at NTI IV), Andy has graduated from most of the major shooting schools in the country (Gunsite, Lethal Force Institute, Yavapai, etc.). He's also achieved a high level of expertise in hand-to-hand combat, including the use of edged weapons. Andy currently serves as a police training instructor in addition to teaching through his own Florida-based school, Options for Personal Security.

Andy trained every member of our department to a skill level that far exceeds that of the average SWAT cop. Being in a multiagency tactical team has some disadvantages, such as the variety of training each officer has or hasn't had. Andy got the team up to par on short notice. One small example is his constant coaching in the Wyatt Protocol. *Fight! Do I need to fight anymore? Do I need to fight anyone else? How do I prepare to fight again?* This SOP helped us be more prepared to handle the violent confrontations a police officer must face from time to time.

I have been training with Andy for several years and have learned material contained in this book firsthand. It has taken me to a new level of shooting skill and a higher level of understanding of the issues involved. When we first met, I was using the Weaver stance as taught at my police academy. After his succinct lecture on the superiority of the modern isosceles, I reluctantly gave it a try. I am not exaggerating when I say my shooting speed increased 100 percent in a month, with a corresponding increase in accuracy. If you are serious about self-defense, you owe it to yourself to give it a fair try too.

As I see it, Andy is 25 percent shooter, 25 percent tactician, 25 percent instructor, and 25 percent scientist. He is equally strong in all of these areas. I know what you are thinking: the scientist part sounds kind of weird. Not really. As Andy considers a new technique, he is very analytical. I'm sure he has a secret room with chemicals bubbling in Pyrex containers and chalkboards with math equations scribbled all over them. He will tear a technique apart to see what it is made of, and only after a lot of trial and error will he incorporate it into his curriculum. He makes these decisions with no ego invested in the techniques he teaches, and he is always open to new ideas. This is a rare trait in the field of professional firearms training, and it is one that keeps Andy and his students on the cutting edge.

James Yeager—"The Lone Wolf of Benton County"—has over a decade of law enforcement experience in undercover, uniformed patrol, and SWAT assignments. An accomplished trainer and author in his own right, he is the former police chief of Big Sandy, Tennessee, and currently serves with a county sheriff's department.

PREFACE

I began my formal combat handgun training in 1977 under the tutelage of Michael Harries—of flashlight technique fame—in the old South West Pistol League founded by Jeff Cooper. For nearly two decades my handgun shooting style of choice was the Weaver stance taught by my Gunsite-trained mentors.

And the Weaver served me well. I used a variant of this stance when I won the 1994 National Tactical Invitational (NTI) at Gunsite Ranch (though photos taken on one stage of the event show me assuming what appears to be a virtually textbook modern isosceles under stress). In short, I was a dyed-in-the-wool Weaver man, and I passionately declaimed that it was the best two-handed shooting stance extant.

At some point after I began teaching firearms skills full time, I softened my position a bit, opining that while Weaver was the best, the isosceles was probably OK too. Then, in the mid-1990s I attended Bill Rogers Institute of Advanced Weaponcraft in Elijay, Georgia. During that course, it became glaringly apparent that the isosceles stance Bill recommended outperformed my well-practiced Weaver by a noticeable margin. The world, it seems, was not flat after all.

Since that first epiphany, I have actively sought out the growing number of other combat firearms instructors who advocate the modern isosceles, and I have read voraciously on the subject. Each of these sources had a different angle on the problem that had to be integrated into the big picture. Eight years experience as a Department of Defense Military Operations Analyst was a great help in this effort.

I continue to study and to learn. That said, what follows covers in detail the major aspects of the topics at hand, in the context of combat as opposed to competition. The methods described herein represent the current state-of-the-art in combat handgunning technique as it exists at this time. May what follows assist you in shooting faster and more accurately when the flag flies, and may it improve your ability to handle your weapon under extreme stress.

SECTION I

INTRODUCTION

Before examining combat handgunning techniques, we must first define exactly what problems they are meant to address. An old adage holds, " If you don't know where you are going, any path will take you there." Hence, in the interest of a well-understood objective, Chapter 1 establishes the goals in question, providing a rationale for the skills covered in Sections II and III.

This section also looks at the history of combat handgunning methods taught in the latter half of the 20th century. We enter the new millennium with techniques that maximize human performance with a sidearm better than ever before, developed largely during the last 50 years. But, as described in Chapter 2, circumstances have conspired to keep these high-speed handgun techniques from achieving their rightful status as state-of-the-art.

1

GOALS AND OBJECTIVES

The purpose of the pistol is to stop fights. It can achieve this through psychological means—via intimidation, either before or after shots are fired—or by inflicting physical effects on an adversary. While the methods discussed in this book will certainly contribute to the former, the bulk of information contained herein relates to terminating hostilities physiologically with gunfire.

But before delving into the techniques required to place hits on target, we should define just what it is we are trying to achieve in the home, on the street, or in the field.

First of all, the physical skills discussed in this book are not performed in a vacuum. Specifically, they must only be

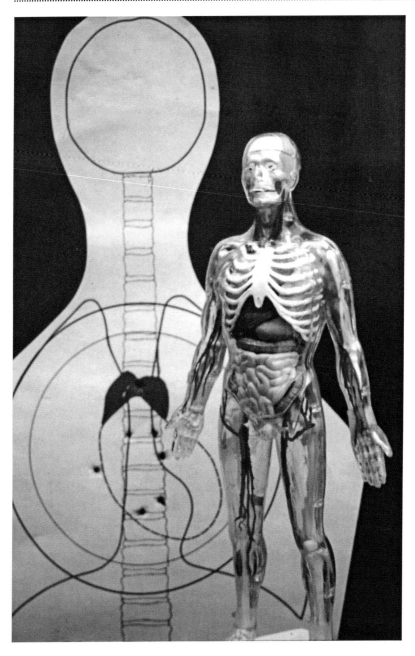

applied in the real world after the moral, ethical, and legal decision to shoot has been made. In a civilian scenario, to include law enforcement scenarios, you are only justified in shooting a person who constitutes (in the words of Massad Ayoob) "an immediate and otherwise unavoidable threat of death or grave bodily harm to an innocent person."

If shooting is required, don't expect miracles. Handgun bullets do not possess magical powers. They merely poke holes in things. The permanent wound track created by the bullet represents the primary means by which any projectile affects a living target. The temporary cavity may damage inelastic tissue such as the liver or brain, but the majority of human tissue will snap back unscathed after the passing of a pistol bullet, except for that tissue actually touched by the projectile.

The only way a bullet can physically cause instantaneous incapacitation is by sufficiently damaging the brain or upper spine. Unfortunately, these targets are difficult to hit in many real-world defensive or tactical situations. Not only do human beings move erratically, but pistol bullets in particular will often glance off of the skull, which, after all, was designed to protect the brain. Putting a round through an eye socket or ear usually does the job, but these are difficult shots to make, especially under stress.

Because the head is so hard to hit, many trainers instead recommend torso shots as a default response when this target is available. Shots that hit the heart and/or aorta are the best way to achieve hypovolemic shock; that is, physical incapacitation that occurs due to lowered blood pressure. Unfortunately this takes time. And even if the heart is completely destroyed, a motivated, goal-oriented, drunk, drugged, or deranged assailant can function for at least several seconds on the oxygen that is already in the brain. An

Left: To physically stop an assailant requires surgical shooting to vital areas of the body. (Andy Stanford)

assailant at contact distance, or one armed with a firearm, can do a lot of damage in that period.

So in reality, instantaneous incapacitation that occurs due to a heart shot is actually a psychological stop. That said, this target is a reasonable compromise, especially considering that centerline hits that penetrate deep may also strike the spine.

Please note that what many people refer to as "center mass" aiming should actually be concerned with hitting the upper chest for maximum probability of damaging the heart. Firing at some nebulous location in the middle of the torso does not teach the proper point of aim for maximum damage to the cardiovascular system: the intersection of the line between the armpits and the body's vertical centerline (i.e., the upper chest).

Viewed from the front, the proper aim point is the center of the triangle bounded by the nipples and the supersternal notch at the base of the throat. Anything outside of this region should be considered a miss. As one of my young colleagues put it: "Sucking chest wounds and gut shots may be painful, but I'll bet having your heart blown through your spine hurts like a bitch too!"

One final means of achieving physical incapacitation with a projectile is to damage or destroy some other part of the body required for fighting. The most common example of this strategy currently being taught—to stop an individual armed with a contact weapon (e.g., knife, club, etc.) from closing distance—is to fire at the pelvic girdle or hip socket. These are reasonable primary targets if your assailant does not possess a firearm, but someone with a gun may still be able to return fire if hit there. Incidentally these below-the-belt anatomical structures are closer to the body's actual "center of mass," which is located approximately 2 inches below the navel.

The bottom line? To physically affect your adversary requires both shot placement and adequate penetration. With proper ammunition, any service-caliber handgun can provide the latter. Hitting the target is up to you. Fist-sized groups at

Service-caliber handgun cartridges (left to right: 9mm Parabellum, .38 Special, .40 S&W, and .45 ACP) are basically equal in terminal effect, given equal shot placement and penetration. Increasing your probability of quickly stopping an assailant requires a centerfire rifle or shotgun (left to right: 5.56 NATO, 7.62 NATO, 12 gauge buckshot, 12 gauge Foster slug). (Andy Stanford)

speed is the goal, since if you can achieve this standard in practice, you will probably still make solid hits under stress. Only when these two conditions have been satisfied do bore diameters and/or bullet expansion come into play.

Which brings us to caliber. Though a slightly larger bullet may very well be marginally more effective, taken in the context of the wound effects discussed above, it actually offers no discernable advantage at service pistol velocities.

Think about it. A .45 ACP is just 0.10 inches greater in diameter than a 9mm/.38. (For readers with math anxiety, this means you can be off target by an additional, whopping 0.05 inches!) An expanding bullet may increase this difference in frontal area a bit more, but even the bigger bullet cannot instantly force an end to the confrontation except by hitting the brain or upper spine. Dr. Mike Shertz, emergency room physician and U.S. Army Special Forces reserve medic, notes that surgeons cannot tell the difference between the wound track from a 9mm/.38 Special and one from a .45. Any increase in blood flow from the wound due to the bigger bullet will be relatively minor in the grand scheme of things. Certainly the end result will be a far cry from the 95 percent instant incapacitation claimed by some trainers for a single torso hit with .45 hardball.

Have no illusions: compared to most centerfire shoulder weapons, any service-caliber auto pistol or revolver is a second-rate firearm to take to a fight. Handguns are certainly portable and concealable, but they are relatively underpowered and difficult to shoot well under stress. In the words of Thunder Ranch Director Clint Smith, "A handgun is what you use to fight your way to your rifle or shotgun." Another top instructor is more blunt: "A handgun is a piece of shit."

In short, the best you can hope for with a handgun is to shoot a hole in an important body part. This in turn requires surgical shot placement. All rounds fired should strike as closely as possible to the desired point(s) of aim. Some instructors promote the idea of "spreading the damage around," but this is unnecessary and will usually be detrimental to good shot placement. The probability that multiple shots will travel along the identical wound track is almost zero, especially given the fact that the target and/or shooter will likely be moving between shots. Hitting a given spot under pressure is hard enough. Why make things more difficult attempting intentional dispersion?

In addition to shooting accurately, you will need to fire as quickly as you can hit. Remember: in a civilian scenario, to include law enforcement shootings, deadly force is only used to counter a similar level of threat. That means someone is trying to kill or maim you, in most cases from a relatively short distance. And he may very well be the one to fire first. Time is usually of the essence in such situations.

An untrained assailant can fire up to four rounds per second. Granted, these probably won't be well-aimed shots, but at close range an opponent doesn't need much skill to hit you. Luck will often suffice. In any case, high-velocity projectiles launched in your direction always represent a greater-than-zero risk of death or crippling injury. Returning accurate fire at a high rate of speed therefore becomes a top priority—in essence achieving fire superiority first, with no misses as your goal.

Even if your opponent is armed with a contact weapon such as a knife or bludgeon, you must be expeditious. The Tueller drill has confirmed time and again that the average person can run 21 feet in less than 2 seconds. At room ranges, your assailant will likely be much closer than that.

Terminating hostilities will often require multiple shots due to the aforementioned terminal ballistics considerations. Additional rounds on target both increase the probability of hitting the intended body part and cause more damage than a single bullet. The quicker you can shoot accurately, the greater the number of effective rounds you can deliver in a given period of time.

When you face more than one assailant, speed becomes even more critical. In such cases, it may be tactically desirable to place one round on each target initially, then engage any remaining threats as necessary on a failure-to-stop basis. Shooting technique plays a definite role in how quickly this can be accomplished.

By the way, since you can't know in advance how many hits will be required to stop a given threat, training to shoot in "double taps," "controlled pairs," or "hammers" can create a potentially dangerous habit: pausing after two rounds have been fired, regardless of the results. Instead, continue shooting as fast as you can hit until the threat goes away, whether this takes one shot, an entire magazine, or every cartridge you carry. In the words of one former lawman, "shoot 'em down to the ground," or until they clearly cease trying to kill or maim you.

For all of the above reasons, you must be able to maximize the number of accurate rounds on target in the time available. You'll also need the ability to shoot effectively with one hand and while moving. Section II (Chapters 3 through 9) contains a detailed explanation of the skills required to accomplish all of these combat marksmanship tasks.

In addition to surgically accurate, high-speed shooting, you must be proficient at effective, efficient, and tactically sound gun handling to get the gun on target quickly and keep it firing throughout the fight. These topics are addressed in Chapters 10, 11, and 12 in a manner that maximizes the probability that the tasks in question can be performed in the extreme stress and chaos of an actual confrontation.

The shooting techniques described herein—and in particular the modern isosceles stance—comprise proven methods of achieving these goals and objectives. The best competitive combat marksmen in the world use them, as do elite military operatives around the globe. However, as we shall see in the next chapter, these methods are not widely understood, even by many who should know better. Hence you will be a member of a select group if you master them.

CHAPTER 2

PISTOL TECHNIQUE IN THE LATE 20ᵀᴴ CENTURY

At the end of World War II, the cutting edge in close-quarters combat handgunning consisted of the point shooting methods formalized by the late Col. Rex Applegate, evolved from those described in *Shooting to Live* by W.E. Fairbairn and E.A. Sykes of the British Shanghai Municipal Police. The FBI, too, taught point shooting for close-range encounters during this period. These methods still deserve study in the context of later developments, particularly for semitrained individuals and in close-quarter, surprise engagments for shooters of any skill level.

Those who desire an in-depth treatment of handgun training in the first half of the century should obtain the book

Quick or Dead by William Cassidy. Colonel Applegate's methods are documented in detail in *Bulleyes Don't Shoot Back*, which he co-authored with my friend Michael Janich. Beginning in the late 1950s, John D. "Jeff" Cooper began holding freestyle combat pistol matches in Big Bear, California. These early shooting competitions were later organized into the South West Pistol League, the direct ancestor of today's International Practical Shooting Confederation (IPSC) and its American counterpart, the United States Practical Shooting Association (USPSA). It quickly became apparent that aimed fire from eye level was the optimum solution to the majority of diverse shooting problems presented on the range.

By observing the shooting styles of the winners of these matches during the 1960s and 1970s, Cooper formalized his "Modern Technique of the Pistol," taught at the American Pistol Institute (API) at Gunsite Ranch, which later became Gunsite Training Center and is currently known as Gunsite Academy. The book *The Modern Technique of the Pistol* by Greg Morrison covers this doctrine in detail. The five elements of Cooper's Modern Technique are the heavy-duty service pistol, the presentation (i.e., draw stroke), the flash sight picture, the compressed surprise trigger break, and the so-called Weaver stance. (I say "so-called" because California Sheriff Jack Weaver's shooting style was a bit different than that taught by Cooper at Gunsite.)

Gunsite started a private sector training revolution, teaching the Modern Technique to thousands of military personnel, police officers, and private citizens worldwide. This doctrine has been passed on to thousands of others via books, videos, magazine articles, and dozens of Gunsite-trained instructors and their schools (e.g., Thunder Ranch, Yavapai Firearms Academy, Range Master, Suarez International, Cumberland Tactics, American Small Arms Academy, Front Sight, etc.)

Of course, not everyone concurred with this view. Point shooting still had its advocates. And gun writer/trainer Massad Ayoob also dissented strongly in his book *Stressfire*. In

Here I am in 1978, when I used the Weaver stance. Note that under the stress of a full surprise tactical shooting exercise, my "Weaver" looks suspiciously like an off-balance isosceles. (Bill Johnson)

lieu of the Weaver stance, Ayoob touted an aggressive, locked-elbow version of the isosceles stance.

Nonetheless, with some conspicuous exceptions, Gunsite-based pistolcraft has dominated private sector defensive and tactical training since the 1970s. On the other hand, the "practical" competitions from which it initially sprang saw the Weaver stance virtually abandoned during the last two decades of the 20th century.

In the early 1980s, Rob Leatham and Brian Enos ascended to the top of the "practical pistol" game. These two young professional marksmen were not wed to any particular shooting style; they were only concerned with besting the competition. Through extensive trial and error during their joint practice sessions, Leatham and Enos arrived at a variation of the isosceles stance described in the following chapters. With a combination of natural talent and groundbreaking technique, they dominated the major match circuit.

Around the same time, 1980 and 1981 IPSC National Champion John Shaw began teaching classes to military special operations forces. He initially used and taught the Weaver stance. But as an active competitive shooter, Shaw soon found himself beaten consistently and decisively by Leatham, Enos, and others who used the modern isosceles. He quickly realized that he would have to abandon the Weaver to keep pace. The change in technique was applied to his school curriculum as well.

Former FBI agent Bill Rogers also taught government personnel during this period, and he went through a similar evolution of methods. Rogers personally began shooting isosceles around 1982, but he continued to teach Weaver for a couple of years after that for purely business reasons: his clients simply wouldn't accept that the isosceles was better. Rogers' school now trains hundreds of military and law enforcement personnel each year in the modern isosceles.

Ironically, the cutting edge shooting techniques described in this book trace their roots to the same source as the Weaver stance (i.e., IPSC/USPSA competition), yet IPSC founder

Colonel Cooper himself scorns them. As one might expect, many of the firearms trainers who got their start at Gunsite take the same position, with an almost religious fervor. Predictably, this includes a significant number of today's top defensive shooting instructors.

Why is this so? In my experience, the people in question are A) largely unaware of the principles and specifics involved with the modern isosceles, and B) not particularly willing to be brought up to speed on the matter. They have also been thoroughly indoctrinated with the message that the classic Modern Technique has no equal, and they do shoot far, far better than the average gun owner. As a result, more than half of the world-class private sector handgun training in this country is still based around the Weaver stance, and the trainers who teach it show no signs of changing their opinions.

Make no mistake: these instructors are not stupid individuals. Many have made great contributions to the field of combat training and continue to do so. Several are friends of mine and are undoubtedly as exasperated at my heretical pronouncements about the modern isosceles as I am about their stubborn insistence that the Weaver stance is still king.

The primary argument advanced by these folks is that one cannot control a big-bore service pistol such as a .45 ACP 1911A1 with service ammo in rapid fire using the isosceles. As a corollary, many Weaver advocates state that the isosceles only works with light loads and/or pistols equipped with muzzle brakes or compensators.

Both of these claims are demonstrably untrue, but even a live-fire demo doesn't seem to carry much weight. Let a Weaver instructor watch an IPSC Grandmaster shooting tight groups from the modern isosceles at six or seven rounds a second, firing a .45 auto with full hardball loads, and the Weaver man (or woman) will protest, "But that individual is a highly trained athlete. The average person can't do that." (I guess the early champions who used the Weaver were not "highly trained athletes.")

This denial in the face of seemingly incontrovertible evidence originates from the very top of the handgunning hierarchy. When IPSC Grandmaster and API graduate Ron Avery won the Gunsite Alumni Shoot—soundly trouncing all comers using the modern isosceles stance and firing an uncompensated, iron-sighted Government Model .45 with full-power ammo—Jeff Cooper dismissed technique as a factor. As he handed Ron the GAS trophy 1911A1 pistol, Cooper remarked, "You just can't beat a man who's naturally fast."

Certainly, many of those who excel using the modern isosceles evince more raw talent than most of us. But the best shooters in the world are not the only ones to shoot isosceles. On the other end of the skill spectrum, videotaped footage of countless actual police shootings shows a large preponderance of the combatants firing from isosceles, if they use both hands at all. This includes officers previously taught the Weaver in academy and/or in-service training.

These results have been replicated time and again under controlled conditions, using Simunition FX paint projectiles in high-level confrontational simulations. During scenarios in which return fire is a factor, shooters generally push both arms out equally when shooting with two hands on the gun. All of this, not coincidentally, is completely consistent with years of study of human motor skills under stress.

For physiological reasons, the isosceles is easier to learn and retain than the Weaver is and therefore is easier to teach. Additionally, the isosceles works much better while shooting on the move due to simple body mechanics. For those who wear protective Kevlar vests, it presents the front panel of the armor squarely to the adversary being addressed. The Weaver stance, on the other hand, exposes more of the side panel seam and unprotected armpit. The directionally neutral isosceles is superior for lateral traverse too, as when engaging multiple threats. And for disciples of Colonel Applegate, it is also a better two-handed stance for point shooting, since it aligns the muzzle better with the body centerline.

Me in the Gunsite "Donga" at the fourth National Tactical Invitational, 1994. Again, my stance looks more like a modern isosceles than a textbook Weaver, but at least it incorporates an aggressive forward lean. (Michelle Miyatake)

As these facts have gained wider acceptance, yet another mantra has become popular among the Weaver crowd: "The modern isosceles may be a better shooting stance, but the Weaver is a better *fighting* stance." This statement confuses foot position with stance per se, a topic discussed in detail in Chapter 4. Suffice to say that a number of isosceles instructors are also black belt martial artists—including Ron Avery, John Holschen, and me—and we feel that the isosceles integrates just fine with our hand-to-hand combat systems.

Along the same lines, Weaver shooters state that their favored pistol technique allows a person to use essentially the same position with a handgun as with a rifle and shotgun. As attractive as this argument may seem, it makes no sense to hamstring one's ability to shoot one type of weapon to the fullest of its capabilities in order to achieve a somewhat dubious commonality with other, fundamentally different weapons. Again, foot position is largely at issue here.

Additionally, and contrary to the above assertion, many military and SWAT operators—including SpecOps hostage rescue teams—have incorporated elements of the modern isosceles into their shoulder weapon stances, taking advantage of the weapon presentation and recoil management concepts in question to get the most out of their MP5s and M4s during high-speed, dynamic engagements.

Note that I am not saying that it's impossible to shoot well from Weaver. I know a number of people who can shoot noticeably better using their Weaveresque stances than I can from the modern isosceles. And several Weaver advocates (Gabe Suarez comes immediately to mind) have used their personal stance to good effect in multiple modern-day gunfights. Weaver shooters who are happy with their skill level—and who don't wish to spend the time, effort, and money on retraining themselves—may very well be better off sticking with what they already know.

That said, the isosceles is clearly technically superior and meets the goals set forth in the previous chapter in a much more natural manner. As shall be evident in the following chapters, the Weaver stance attempts a brute force solution while the modern isosceles "goes with the flow." To claim that Weaver represents the zenith of combat pistol technique is simply untrue, nothing more than dogmatic dinosaur doctrine. Refusing to devote sufficient unbiased study to the matter clearly indicates nothing less than old-fashioned close mindedness. Given that the isosceles is both a natural reaction among the semitrained *and* the overwhelming choice of world class marksmen, doesn't it at least bear an objective, closer look?

Perhaps less controversial than the modern isosceles stance, our understanding of efficient and tactically sound gun handling has also increased dramatically in the last decades. These techniques were largely developed by the private sector training community as opposed to the aforementioned competitive shooters who refined the isosceles stance.

A critical element of skill at arms, practiced and proper gun handling represents a major factor in one's overall combat capability with a firearm. It has a great impact on how quickly you can engage a threat with gunfire, as much so as the speed at which you can aim and control your trigger.

Specifically, the ability to bring the weapon to bear from the holster or suitable ready position in an expeditious manner can play a significant role in your survival. Rapidly reloading and clearing malfunctions under stress are also potentially life-saving skills. Our knowledge of how to best accomplish these gunfighting tasks is greater than ever, and this topic is covered in the last three chapters.

As a student of weaponcraft, you have probably encountered some of these techniques and concepts before. On the other hand, if you have been taught by an instructor who advocates the Weaver stance or have no formal training at all, much of what follows may be entirely new to you. But whether a relative neophyte or an experienced hand—or even a Weaver shooter—you will get the most out of this book if you keep an open mind. Now, on to specifics.

SECTION II

THE POSTMODERN TECHNIQUE OF THE PISTOL

The next seven chapters cover the motor skills that comprise the cutting edge in combat pistol marksmanship methods. Although members of the "gamesman" faction of IPSC/USPSA initially developed many of these techniques, they have been proven in combat as well as in competition. To ignore the modern isosceles because of its origins would be foolish at the very least.

Based on sound principles of physics and human physiology, the techniques themselves are quite common sense. Most evolved from time-tested shooting fundamentals, and many of the concepts can be used to enhance a Weaver stance as well. With sufficient practice and expert execution, each element combines synergistically with the others to facilitate truly amazing levels of practical pistol prowess.

CHAPTER
3
GRIP

Your grip on the pistol is the direct interface between human and weapon. It provides a means of aligning the pistol with the target, both holding it steady on target for visually verified aiming and providing a tactile indication of the direction in which the handgun is pointed. Your grip also stabilizes the weapon against poor trigger control and is a major factor in recoil management.

With the modern isosceles, as with the Weaver, the dominant hand should grip the weapon as high as practical relative to the bore line of the weapon in order to limit muzzle flip. This means the web of the hand should be snug against the top of the tang or grip safety on a semiautomatic pistol and approximately even with the top of the backstrap on a wheelgun. The fingers should be kept together, not splayed out, and should make contact with the frame as high as possible, with the middle finger snug against the bottom of the trigger guard on an auto loader.

The oft-repeated advice of aligning the bore with the firing hand forearm doesn't apply with the modern isosceles. In the two-handed stance described in this section, the recoil should come straight back toward the shooter's dominant eye, to distribute the force down both arms as equally as possible. Hence the bore line will be inward of the dominant side arm as viewed from above.

Additionally, shooters with small hands often have difficulty reaching the trigger when the barrel is directly in line with the forearm. Since trigger control is key to good marksmanship—and more of a problem for most shooters than aiming the weapon or recoil control—it's generally better to start with the desired trigger finger placement and work backwards.

Placement of the index finger on the trigger is a subject of debate even among expert shooters. Master marksmen do good work with a variety of trigger finger placements, ranging from somewhere on the first pad back to the first joint from the tip. There is a tradeoff here between sensitivity (pad of the finger) and leverage (first joint). Hence those with relatively light triggers, including most top competitive shooters, tend to use the pad.

In any case, you must be able to comfortably reach the trigger. Thus finger length will play a major role in where you place your trigger finger, as does the distance from tang or backstrap—where the web of the shooting hand contacts the gun—to the face of the trigger. The knuckle joint at the base of the index finger should remain stationary when the trigger is manipulated. Whatever part of the finger you use, it should contact the trigger face only, ideally in the center, and never touch the side of the trigger or frame of the gun.

The firing hand thumb should still be kept as high as possible. (Clay Babcock)

Obviously, the size and shape of the weapon in question will affect the ultimate results that can be achieved. Many guns are simply too big for shooters with small hands, particularly double-action auto pistols with double-column magazines. For the same reason, most people are well advised to avoid accessories such as the rubber "Glock sock," which increase the girth of their weapon.

With autos, keep the firing hand thumb high, positioning the web of the hand as close as possible to the bore line and creating room for the support hand. With a single-action self-loader with a frame-mounted safety (e.g., the 1911A1 or P35), rest your thumb on the safety lever. In addition to providing a high grip, resting your thumb on the safety ensures that you will disengage it as the weapon is brought to bear from the holster or ready position. It also prevents you from inadvertently engaging the safety under recoil.

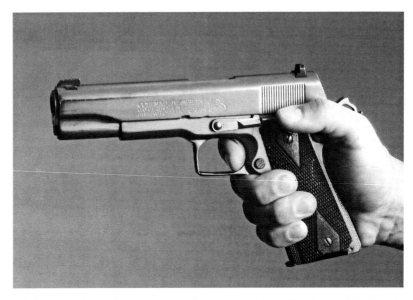

With a 1911A1-style single-action auto pistol, the dominant side thumb should rest on the safety. (Clay Babcock)

Due to the physical structure of the weapon, revolver shooters are generally better off with a low firing-hand thumb placement, with the tip of the thumb touching the tip of the firing hand middle finger. Wheelgun wizard Jerry Miculek shoots this way.

Wrap your support hand around the front of the weapon and over the dominant hand, with the fingers on each hand roughly parallel to each other, and again as high as possible. As with the dominant hand, fingers on the support hand should be kept together, not splayed out, with the index finger snug against the bottom of the trigger guard.

Although many handguns feature a squared and/or checkered trigger guard, your grip will generally be weaker if you place your support hand index finger there. Jerry Barnhart is the only top IPSC Grandmaster to put his support

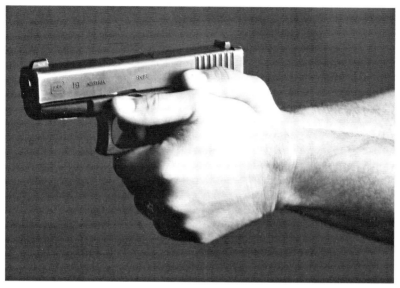

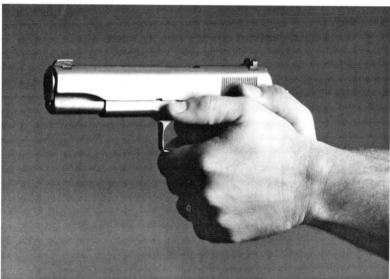

The modern isosceles grip places the support hand thumb under the dominant hand thumb for maximum hand-to-gun contact. (Clay Babcock)

hand index finger on the trigger guard. This may increase tactile indication of weapon alignment, but as noted, most do otherwise. Even Barnhart recommends that his students put their index fingers underneath instead of mimicking his grip.

Angle the support hand downward. If you were to open this hand, the fingers should point approximately 30 to 45 degrees below horizontal. This raises the base of the support hand thumb, allowing this point of maximum skin contact to be positioned as high as possible relative to the bore line, minimizing the leverage exerted by recoil. The friction this part of your hand provides against the side of the weapon contributes significantly to recoil management. Camming the support side hand downward also assists in "locking" the wrist, described in the next chapter. The position of your support hand thumb is largely irrelevant. I point mine toward the target.

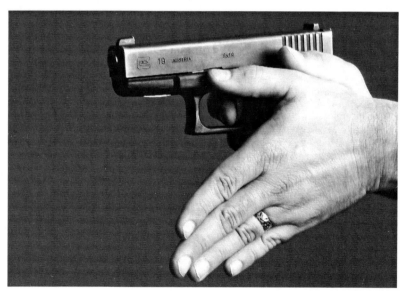

To check for proper support hand placement, open the hand and note if the fingers are pointed downward. (Clay Babcock)

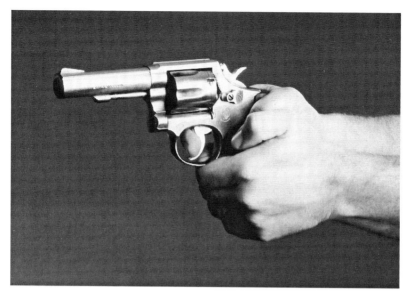

A thumb-over-thumb grip is generally used with a revolver due to the ergonomics of this type of weapon. (Clay Babcock)

On an auto pistol, place the support thumb under the dominant side thumb, with the base of the support hand's first metacarpal (i.e., wrist end of thumb edge of hand) nestled into the joint where the dominant thumb meets the hand (i.e., at the head, or distal end, of the dominant hand's first metacarpal). At this point the handle of the gun should be completely surrounded with flesh, with no gap between your two thumbs.

With a revolver, place the support side thumb over the dominant side thumbnail. The support hand fingers won't point down as much when shooting a wheelgun, again due to the physical structure of the weapon. Some people cross the support side thumb around the backstrap and over the web of the dominant hand. While not recommended, you can get away with this when firing a revolver; doing so with an auto pistol is not only poor technique but dangerous as well.

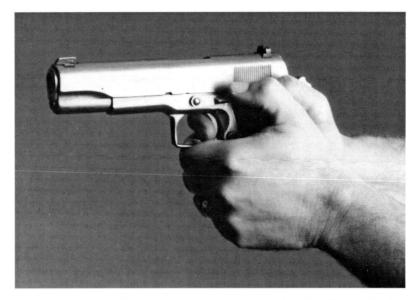

The API/Gunsite school grip places the support hand thumb over the firing hand thumb, creating a gap. (Clay Babcock)

Both the Gunsite school grip and Ayoob's Stressfire system teach a thumb-over-thumb grip with both revolver and auto pistol. This creates a gap on the support hand side of the grip, with no hand contact at this point, which diminishes control of the pistol. Hence the high thumbs grip is a superior method with an auto.

With either action type, the support hand squeezes the sides of the pistol, like a clamshell or C-clamp. This will assist in directing the recoil forces straight back and straight up, making the recoil cycle consistent and therefore predictable. This is a key element of the modern isosceles stance.

The support hand exerts more force on the weapon than the dominant hand. Some trainers describe this as a 60/40 percent distribution, or even 70/30. The support hand palm presses the dominant hand fingertips onto the gun. The support hand does the lion's share of the work, allowing the

A thumb over thumbnail grip creates a gap on the support side of the weapon as well. (Clay Babcock)

dominant hand to be relatively relaxed for increased trigger finger sensitivity and speed. It also prevents "trigger freeze," which occurs due to not letting the trigger travel far enough forward to reset in rapid fire, a result of mental and physical tension. Part of this additional support hand effort is a natural consequence of the fact that it wraps around both the gun and the dominant hand, just as more force is required to grip the large end of a baseball bat as tightly as the small end.

If you can get the back edge of the support hand slightly behind the pistol, so much the better, since this will provide an additional buttress against recoil. Otherwise, recoil will be transmitted to the support hand solely by friction between that hand and the side of the gun and between the support hand and dominant hand. Ideally, your hands should mate just forward of the wrists, on the support side at the back of the pistol.

The support hand palm should buttress the backstrap of the pistol. (Clay Babcock)

Whereas the Weaver stance emphasizes push-pull isometric tension—dominant side arm pushing forward, support arm pulling back—in the modern isosceles both arms push the pistol away from the shooter, opposite recoil and toward the target. Instead of trying to fight against the effects of recoil like the Weaver stance, the modern isosceles seeks to manage it in a consistent manner in order to minimize variation between shots.

Recoil and muzzle flip can never be completely eliminated, and attempting to overcome these forces by brute strength takes a toll on other important shooter attributes. In any case, with a proper grip and modern isosceles stance, it's simply unnecessary to struggle.

4 | STANCE

For our purposes here, stance is defined as the position of your body from the arms down to the feet—in short, everything except your grip on the weapon. In this chapter, stance will be broken down into the lower half of the body and the upper half. Let's start at the bottom.

How you stand always involves a trade-off between stability and mobility. A wide stance, such as a martial arts "horse stance," creates a stable base but requires a significant weight shift before you can move. On the other hand placing the feet directly together, as in a ballerina's "first position," facilitates quick movement while creating a lack of stability akin to that of a bowling pin. Most firearms trainers recom-

With the modern isosceles stance, the best natural point of aim will generally be achieved with a slightly off-square foot position, dominant side foot back. (Clay Babcock)

mend a position with feet approximately shoulder width apart, assuming this is possible in a specific scenario.

Foot placement determines stance integrity in a given direction. You can best resist force in the direction of a line drawn between the feet. This is why you drop one foot back when pushing a heavy object and why fencers place their feet roughly on the line between themselves and their opponents. Conversely, any force perpendicular to this line will easily move you.

From a pure shooting standpoint, the optimum foot placement is one that results in a natural point of aim with no excessive muscle tension. Grip on the weapon and the relative bend in each arm determine where the feet will be to achieve this. When holding the pistol with two hands as described in the previous chapter, the support hand wrist will be slightly forward of the firing side wrist. Hence extending both arms equally—as will generally be the case under the stress of a life-threatening event—pulls the support side arm and shoulder forward, which rotates the torso, pulling the hip forward, and so on, ultimately pulling the support side foot forward slightly, with the heel of this foot approximately even with the middle of the dominant side foot (i.e., the dominant side foot slightly back). Coupled with the slight forward over-balance discussed later, this slightly off-square orientation will provide enough counteracting pressure to resist the recoil of any service-caliber handgun.

In close-quarters combat, however, it may be desirable to drop the dominant side foot back a bit further, providing greater stance integrity toward the front. Remember, at short range you may have to transition quickly from shooting to hand-to-hand combat. A compromise foot placement that supports fighting in general will often serve you better than one optimized for shooting only. In other words, you may not want to stand as square to the target as required by your true natural point of aim. This will require that you rotate at the knees and/or waist to bring the gun back on target; doing the

The dominant side foot can be dropped back more for increased stance
integrity to the front during close-quarters combat. (Clay Babcock)

former will keep your hips square to the target and is there-fore preferred.

On the other hand, avoid an extremely bladed stance, i.e., with both feet touching the imaginary line between you and the primary threat. Many Weaver shooters drop the domi-nant foot back excessively, as if on a surfboard or tightrope. Such a position requires excessive muscle tension to bring the gun on target, particularly with both arms extended in an isosceles stance.

Shooting from a bladed stance, you will tend to "unwind" in the direction of the rearmost foot and toward your natural point of aim with each shot. You'll therefore have to exert energy to keep the gun on target. When firing multiple shots rapidly, this will cause rounds to string laterally on target, since your ability to compensate will be overcome by the cumulative effect of each successive recoil impulse. A bias to one side also affects your ability to traverse the gun.

The position of the arms and grip characteristics actually define the type of shooting stance in question. I frequently hear people say things like, "I stand Weaver," or "I place my feet in an isosceles position." In reality, either technique can be assumed with any type of foot placement. Isosceles shoot-er Jerry Barnhart orients his feet approximately 45 degrees to the firing line, a classic "Weaver" foot position.

In any case, the ultimate goal of any stance is balance, and most defensive or tactical scenarios will require move-ment, making static foot placement a moot point. To facilitate this movement while maintaining balance and minimizing the effects of recoil, shoot from the body's "natural action stance." Face the target more or less squarely, with your dominant side foot slightly back. Bend your knees, but do not crouch excessively.

Before dissecting the top end of the modern isosceles stance, let's take a quick look at the Weaver stance and why it doesn't hold together as well in rapid fire. First of all, we have to define what is meant by "Weaver" stance. Most

Gunsite-trained instructors would probably agree with the following: dominant arm more or less straight, support arm more bent with the elbow pointing downward, and push-pull isometric tension between the hands for the purpose of controlling muzzle flip.

Not everything that looks like a Weaver stance meets the preceding definition. For instance, it is clearly impossible to pull back with the support hand while moving it forward. Therefore, in a maximum speed draw, with the shot breaking immediately upon weapon alignment, there is no isometric tension between the hands at the moment of weapon discharge. Is this still a Weaver? This observation gives rise to the question: what do you call such a stance without push-pull tension?

One major drawback to the Weaver is that it is asymmetrical. As noted in the previous chapter, a pistol will recoil toward the path of least resistance. In the Weaver, recoil—rearward along the bore line—travels primarily down the straightened dominant arm. Since the bore line is above the hand, some recoil gets translated into muzzle flip. In a misguided attempt to limit this, the Weaver shooter pulls the support hand back against the dominant.

The support arm, pulling back, actually exerts force in the same general direction as the recoil itself. Hence the gun recoils up and toward the dominant side and must be brought back to bear by muscle. The degree to which this can be achieved consistently is far less with a Weaver than with a symmetrical stance that uses natural point of aim. At maximum speed, the cumulative effect of this variation between shots causes a significant increase in group size. In many ways, the Weaver has the negative attributes of shooting with one hand unsupported.

Additionally, the relatively high degree of tension in the body with the Weaver has a detrimental effect on trigger control, recoil management (discussed below), and performance in general. Think about it. Can you name any other psychomotor skill in which an instructor would recommend the

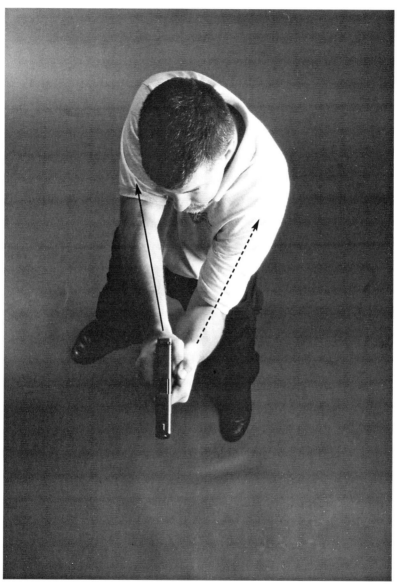

In a Weaver stance, recoil forces travel primarily down the firing side arm. (Clay Babcock)

In the modern isosceles stance, recoil forces travel more or less equally down both arms. (Clay Babcock)

student to constantly tense up? On the contrary, coaches in a host of physical endeavors have to frequently remind their students to "relax." The brute force approach taken by a Weaver shooter is not the best way to manage recoil. These folks fight to bring the weapon back on target each time the gun discharges. Perhaps the muzzle rises a bit less due to these exertions, but the price paid far outweighs any benefits. The effort spent on this constant struggle takes mental energy that could be better applied to aiming, trigger control, and tactics. (Lately, some instructors have been promoting a "relaxed Weaver." This is clearly neither fish nor fowl.)

Weaver instructors clearly do not understand the following: the amount of muzzle flip per se is not the primary factor in quick shot-to-shot recovery. Rather, when the next round can be accurately fired is determined primarily by how quickly and consistently the muzzle returns to the same position. It is therefore desirable to create a neutral body structure behind the gun that controls and dissipates the recoil forces to achieve this goal. The modern isosceles accomplishes this much better than the Weaver, with far less effort on the part of the shooter, and in a manner consistent with human performance under extreme stress.

This brings us to the heart of the matter: the modern isosceles from the wrists backwards to the waist. The wrists should be "locked" into position to minimize vertical stringing. Technically, one does not actually lock the wrist joints; instead, the tendons are tensed to hold the wrists stable. (This is how a bird sleeps on a wire, using tendon strength.) You should feel as if you are camming the pistol downwards. The muscles in your forearms control these tendons and therefore will be taut.

To test your ability to accomplish this "lock," simulate your grip on the weapon (with no gun) while a training partner faces you, places his hands around yours, and attempts to bend your wrists up and down. Keep your hands in consistent alignment with your arms. This is the desired tension.

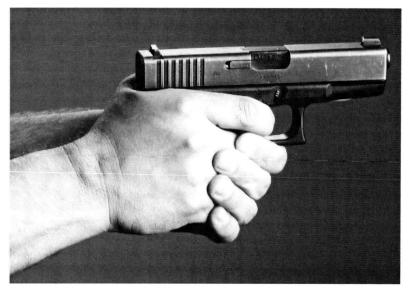

The tendons in the wrists should be taut, "locking" this joint in position. (Clay Babcock)

With the wrists stabilized in this manner—and the rest of your stance correct—the pistol should snap back into position automatically after recoil. You may notice more muzzle flip than with a Weaver stance, but the sights will nonetheless return quickly and precisely to your pre-discharge point of aim, and without any additional effort on your part. This can be critical in close-range fights, during which people tend to pull the trigger as quickly as they can once the weapon is brought to bear.

Your arms should be as symmetrical as possible to create a neutral resistance to recoil. Different shooters extend their arms to varying degrees, but you should not lock them out completely. Though locked-out arms are still superior to the Weaver, this is not your position of greatest strength. A good starting place is the natural extension achieved when carrying a heavy suitcase. IPSC ace Jerry "Burner" Barnhart bends his arms a bit more and feels that

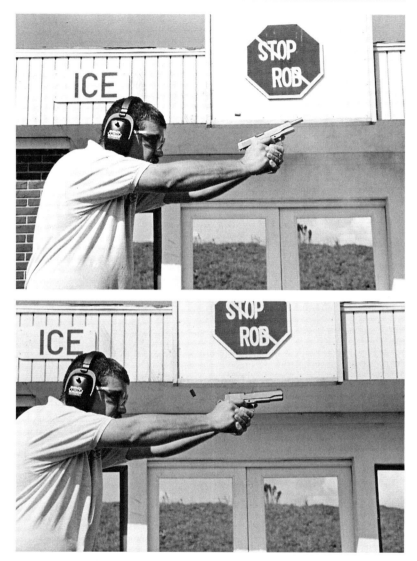

The amount of muzzle flip is largely irrelevant, provided the gun returns consistently to the original point of aim. These photos are from a sequence of shots fired with hardball .45 ACP loads at sub 0.20 second splits between rounds, all of which hit in the "A" zone of an IPSC silhouette at 7 yards. (Eleanor Stanford)

he dissipates more of the recoil energy this way. You may wish to experiment and note the effect on recoil management.

Fully locked-out arms, with hyperextended elbows, will allow the recoil forces to batter your elbow joints. This can be painful in the short term, akin to tennis elbow, and potentially damaging over time. Recovering Weaver shooters may tend to bend the support side arm more than the dominant arm at first, and when learning the isosceles

IPSC Grandmaster Ron Avery demonstrates the modern isosceles. Note that Ron's shoulders are relatively relaxed and both arms significantly bent. This is the textbook upper body position used by all top competitive "practical pistol" shooters.

they may need to initially lock out their arms in order to achieve true symmetry. If you're one of these people, make this transitional phase as brief as possible to save wear and tear on your elbows.

Ideally, your upper arms and shoulders should be relaxed, pushing outward with the shoulders slightly adducted. When you are tense, the recoil rebounds, much like a tennis ball bouncing off a brick wall (another reason not to hyperextend your elbows). With the shoulders relaxed, much of the energy is absorbed, analogous to throwing the tennis ball into a pile of sand. The photo of IPSC Grandmaster Ron Avery illustrates a fairly ideal shoulder position for maximum high-speed marksmanship.

That said, in combat, the human fight-or-flight response often produces a hunching of the shoulders to protect the neck and throat. While suboptimal from a pure shooting standpoint, this instinctive protection is not an entirely bad thing for overall survivability, particularly in a short-range fight against multiple assailants. As with many tactical factors, it involves a trade-off.

To counteract recoil, it is also desirable to create a slight overbalance forward, enhancing the contribution of your body weight. Although the recoil impulse of a given handgun round is not that great, the cumulative force of firing rapid, multiple shots has a significant impact on shot-to-shot recovery. At maximum speed, the effect is analogous to the torquing recoil of a submachine gun, though not quite as great since your rate of fire will be lower.

Bend progressively forward, with your chin ahead of your toes and your head in front of your torso. The photos in this chapter should give you some idea of what this should look like. You should feel as if you are leaning into a strong headwind. If your butt sticks out, you're probably crouching to maintain balance; straighten your knees a bit and jack knife at the waist instead, rounding your torso.

Top competitive shooters achieve just enough lean to overcome the kickback of their specific weapon. You may need to exaggerate this aspect of your stance initially, gradually fine tuning it over time. Needless to say, standing straight up—or worse, leaning backward—will be detrimental to performance when firing more than one shot. Even the relatively mild recoil of a service pistol can rock you back on your heels when firing at maximum speed due to the cumulative effect of multiple rapid shots. Note that this forward overbalance can also facilitate using hand-to-hand techniques against a contact-distance assailant.

When viewed from above, your head should not be tilted to the side, since this places you out of balance, a state determined by the orientation of the inner ear. This is particularly apparent when moving: just try walking quickly through a cluttered area with your head cocked over.

Many older shooters suffer from presbyopia, a gradual hardening of the lens of the eye which leads to an inability to

Above and next page: Many combat firing positions look nothing like a textbook isosceles or Weaver. (Clay Babcock)

focus on close objects, such as the front sight of a handgun. These people will often tip their heads backward in order to see the sights clearly through the lower lens of their bifocals. Obviously, this works against the goal of forward balance. Also, the sight may be clear but nothing else will be! As noted in the next chapter, perfect sight focus is unnecessary at common self-defense distances as long as you can see what's necessary to align weapon and target.

Speaking of vision, ideally both eyes should be open when you shoot, but many people squint or even close one eye when firing. If you're one of these folks, don't be overly concerned. Yes, peripheral vision will suffer with one eye closed, but while shooting your attention will be on your gun/sights and the target anyway. Exactly how you accomplish this visual verification of alignment is unimportant, and your brain will usually take care of things just fine on its own.

In addition to its physical aspects, a forward stance projects an aggressive body language that can contribute to the overall outcome of a fight. The majority of human communication occurs through nonverbal means; the words you say and the tone of voice with which you say them are less than half the message.

The sum total of the elements of the modern isosceles stance achieves the following. Grip on the weapon, in concert with a symmetrical position of the arms, channels recoil forces into a predictable, repeatable path. The wrists, elbows, and shoulders attenuate these forces while minimizing recovery time caused by rebounding energy. And the entire body is balanced in the direction of the target, using mass to counter overall recoil impulse.

Of course, real-world scenarios will often require that you assume shooting positions that bear little resemblance to a textbook standing isosceles. In some cases (e.g., when kneeling behind low horizontal cover), you may be able to incorporate most of the elements described above. In other situations—for instance, a right-handed shooter firing out the driver's side window toward the side or rear of the vehicle—a Weaver-type stance may be necessary. Ultimately, stance is just a means to an end. The modern isosceles may achieve this end in an optimal fashion, but this ideal solution may not be possible in some situations. You may have to fire from an unconventional position to maximize use of cover or to bring the muzzle to bear after being knocked to the ground. You may have to shoot with one hand unsupported, while moving, or while using a flashlight. In so doing, application of the principles in the following chapters can assist you in achieving surgical shooting under adverse conditions.

CHAPTER 5 | AIMING

In simplest terms, hitting a specific target with the projectile from a firearm requires that the firearm be held so that the trajectory coincides sufficiently with the intended point of impact at the moment the projectile leaves the barrel.

The above description may be a bit verbose, but it defines the problem without tying it to a particular solution. Aligning trajectory and target—i.e., aiming—is the subject of this chapter. Ensuring that sufficient weapon alignment is maintained until the bullet leaves the barrel will largely be a matter of trigger control, addressed in Chapter 6.

Historically, aiming with iron sights has been taught as optically superimposing correct sight alignment on the target, resulting in a proper sight picture. Since sight alignment creates angular errors, the proper relationship of front and rear sight usually receives plenty of attention during firearms training. Additionally, students are told over and over again about the importance of focusing on the front sight.

The textbook description of open sight aiming—front sight centered in the rear sight notch, tip of the front sight level with the top of the rear sight, the shooter focusing on the former—will certainly facilitate hitting the intended target. However, it is a bit limiting, often overly precise, and frequently too slow for combat applications.

The vast majority of fights involving pistols occur at conversational range, many at contact distance. At close quarters a bullseye sight picture is just not necessary. Yes, shooting someone with a handgun will at times require extreme precision. An adversary at long range, or one who exposes only a small part of his body from behind cover, comes immediately to mind. In these situations, hitting will require that the shooter confirm that the sights are very well aligned. However, most scenarios demand less precision and commensurately more speed.

In any case, you might be surprised at the level of accuracy that can be achieved without a perfect sight picture. For instance, did you know that it is possible to make head shots at 7 yards—across a large room—with grossly misaligned sights? You can prove this to yourself by firing a group as follows: one round with the front sight perfectly located in the rear notch, one with the edge of the front sight touching one side of the notch, one with other edge of the front sight against the other side of the notch, one with the tip of the front sight barely showing above the bottom of the notch, and one with the front sight high by a commensurate amount. Hold the tip of the front sight on the same spot for every shot. Provided you manage your trigger adequately, the group should be no more than 4 inches in diameter.

A textbook sight picture is often not necessary to achieve surgical shooting. This target shows the results of five chest shots slow fire from 15 yards with a Glock 17 with sights removed and five head shots timed fire (0.5 seconds between shots) using a Glock 19 equipped with Ashley Big Dot Tritium Express sights. (Andy Stanford)

Likewise, it is possible to see the sights and note their alignment with your focus on the target or somewhere between the front sight and target. Yes, the sights will be somewhat blurry, but if they offer sufficient contrast, they will still provide the information you need to make the hit. Certainly you should be able to note excessively misaligned sights. Given that your natural tendency under duress will be to look at the threat anyway, this type of aiming is a very useful combat skill.

Shifting your focus toward the target also yields great benefits in situational awareness. Try this experiment when driving.

First, make sure the road is straight and there is no traffic. Next, focus on a spot on the windshield. Notice how your awareness of the overall environment decreases. Now shift your focus out just a bit beyond the glass; your awareness should expand significantly. I would argue that narrowing your attention could be at least as detrimental during a violent confrontation. (If I were to recommend a martial arts technique that required you to focus hard on your thumbnail during the confrontation, you'd probably decline to use it, and rightly so.)

At sufficiently close range you can even use the outline of the rear of the gun as your "sight" (i.e., Jim Cirillo's "silhouette point" technique). If you see the top or side of the gun, you know it is tilted up or to one side respectively. Conversely, if everything looks symmetrical, the bore is probably aligned well enough with the target to make a good hit at room ranges.

Tactile confirmation of weapon alignment, i.e., by "feel," is another valuable source of information. The thinner the pistol in question, the better the directional information it provides. Hence single-stack auto pistols offer better feedback in this regard than those with double column magazines. Weapon alignment by feel can work in conjunction with the "silhouette point" aiming described above to increase precision under low light conditions. With "sight alignment" confirmed by feel, superimposing the gun on target achieves "sight picture." The more natural body alignment of the isosceles stance, relative to the Weaver, helps greatly here.

In short, front sight focus is unnecessary in close-range combat handgun scenarios, and attempting to obtain a perfect sight picture for every shot under such conditions will often slow you down to an unacceptable degree. The weapon aiming reference that intersects the eye-to-target line can range from barest recognition that the weapon has intersected this line—as in the eye level Applegate technique—to textbook sight alignment and front sight focus. Learn what constitutes an acceptable sight picture for different situations.

The bottom line is to see what *you* need to see to make the hit. An accomplished shooter can get away with far less sight focus than a neophyte. However, except when literally at arm's length, it is desirable to look *for* the sights, even if the situation does not require that you look directly *at* the sights. Beginning and intermediate shooters are well advised to concentrate on the front sight and its position relative to the rear sight, since this is the first step in the process of developing the ability to "feel" when the weapon is aligned. The front sight in particular is a valuable reference, being located just above the point where the bullet will exit the gun. Letting your focus drift downrange while remaining aware of sight picture is an advanced skill.

Don't kid yourself: you need a definite source of weapon alignment information. Yes, you can attain a high degree of tactile awareness of boreline orientation. How you learn this skill is the issue. Short of expending an inordinate amount of ammunition in a trial and error training process, the sights will provide a significant percentage of this feedback in practice. In other words, a textbook sight picture can serve as "training wheels," a visual template that can train your body to align the gun with the target when you can't (or don't) see the sights clearly. Once again, you must walk before you can run.

And remember: even if you don't see your sights, you *must* positively identify your target. It may indeed be possible to shoot at a sound and hit the source, but the legal and moral aspect of threat identification—as stated in Gunsite safety rule #4: "Be sure of your target and what is beyond it"—militate strongly against such actions. In all cases, you must confirm that the person you are shooting constitutes, again as Massed Ayoob puts it, "an immediate and otherwise unavoidable threat of death or grave bodily injury to an innocent person."

To get quicker at visually verified aiming, you will have to get quicker at seeing the relationship of gun and target. Human vision can identify approximately 30 distinct images

The AO Express Big Dot tritium sight facilitates the quickest possible front sight acquisition, even with your eyes focused on the threat. (Clay Babcock)

per second. You can't pull the trigger that many times during the same period, and in any event the weapon will not cycle that quickly. Hence, with sufficient practice, you can become quite adept at confirming an acceptable sight picture as you fire. As you gain experience, you will actually see things faster.

A good test of your current abilities in this area is to watch for your ejecting brass if you shoot an auto pistol. If you can see the empty case come out of the gun, you have a fairly high "see speed." Note that this may require that you bring your focus in closer than your front sight.

A couple of sight options can assist you in seeing more quickly. First of all, you can widen the rear notch with conventional square notch-and-post open sights, increasing the "light bars" on either side of the front sight and giving your sight picture more contrast. The more contrast, the less direct focus will be required to perceive the relationship of the front and rear sights.

Some shooters worry that this modification will affect precision. Remember, a combat pistol is primarily a short-range defensive instrument and should logically be optimized for this task as opposed to long-range target shooting. In any case, a high-contrast sight picture may actually result in increased practical accuracy at speed, since the shooter will see the sights more clearly.

A second option, one that I have installed on all of my defensive handguns, is the AO Express Sight designed by Ashley Emerson and consisting of a shallow "V" rear sight and large, round, white front sight. I prefer the Big Dot tritium version for maximum probability of seeing my front sight under conditions that may induce extreme stress (e.g., someone at close range trying to kill me.)

Because the rear sight does not obscure the large front bead, the AO Express sight picture greatly emphasizes the latter. These sights are very easy to acquire visually and are particularly well-suited to dynamic situations in which the shooter is moving. And as with a widened rear sight notch, the AO Express Sight provides plenty of precision. Once the correct sight picture is understood, it is no problem to make head shots at 25 yards if the shooter is up to the task.

Note that the majority of fights occur not only at close range but in dim light or darkness as well. Huge and white, with a self-luminous insert in the center, the AO Big Dot tritium front sight is optimized for such conditions. It represents nothing less than a revolutionary advance in combat handgun sighting systems.

Whatever sights you use, or even if you depend primarily on tactile confirmation of weapon alignment, most shooters can line up the bore with a vital area of their adversary with adequate precision, given enough time. But the projectile will not hit the intended point of impact unless you maintain this alignment as you fire the gun. This is the topic of trigger control—covered in the next chapter—and for most shooters it represents the key to marksmanship.

6 | TRIGGER CONTROL

Of all the factors that come into play in placing a single accurate shot on target, trigger control seems to cause the most difficulty for the largest number of shooters. In fact, the difference between a good marksman and someone who can't hit the proverbial "bull in the ass with a bass fiddle" almost always boils down to a matter of trigger control.

The last chapter began by defining the requirements for placing a single shot on target. Recall that not only must the weapon be properly aligned with the intended point of impact, but this alignment must also be maintained until the projectile leaves the barrel of the weapon. Attaining a sufficient alignment (i.e., aiming) is generally much easier than

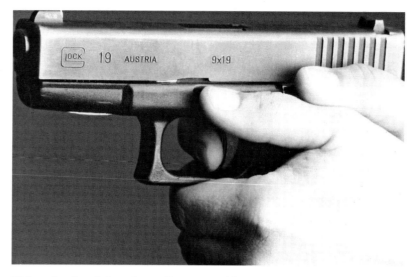

Using the tip of the trigger finger provides maximum sensitivity. (Clay Babcock)

causing the weapon to discharge (i.e., manipulating the trigger) without disturbing that aim.

The key to trigger control is to move *only* the distal end of the trigger finger when pressing or stroking the trigger. Note that I did not use the word "squeeze," as this connotes the use of the entire hand, as in squeezing a lemon, or the thumb and forefinger in opposition, as in squeezing an eyedropper. Instead, with a single-action auto pistol or similar trigger action (e.g., Glock), think of pressing the trigger like a button on a computer keyboard. With a double-action trigger, whether on a revolver or double-action-only (DAO) self-loader, think of stroking the trigger: one smooth, continuous motion.

The variables that must be controlled vis-a-vis the index finger are A) the direction in which pressure is applied to the trigger, B) how much pressure is applied, and C) how that pressure is applied over time. Common sense tells us that to maintain weapon alignment, our manipulation of the trigger

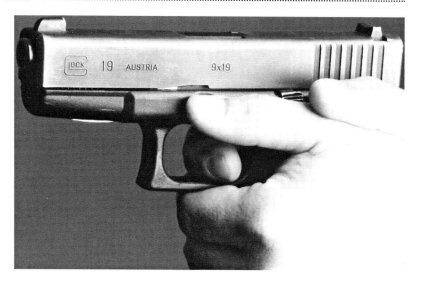

Using the first joint of the trigger finger provides increased leverage. (Clay Babcock)

must not push or pull the gun to one side or the other. Hence the trigger must be pressed or stroked straight to the rear. It may help here to think of moving the trigger straight back toward your shooting eye.

Let's look at how pressure should be applied to the trigger. As discussed in Chapter 1, close-quarters combat shooting often entails firing multiple rounds as quickly as one can hit. Under these circumstances, the shooter will know exactly when the weapon will discharge, precluding a "surprise trigger break," even one compressed in time. Shots at extended distances, a relative rarity in pistol fights, may allow you a bit more time to press or stroke the trigger, but these are the exception, not the rule. In any case, we are talking here about situations in which "slow fire" may very well be as fast as one shot per second.

Even so, do not simply slap the trigger. You may get away with this at close range, particularly when firing a 1911A1-

type auto pistol with a sub-5-pound trigger. But with a heavier street trigger you will likely jerk the gun off target at much beyond arm's length. Yes, a lighter pull is easier to overcome without disturbing weapon alignment, but you really don't need the light, crisp trigger of a custom single-action semiauto to shoot well. With proper trigger manipulation you can shoot about as well using any reasonable handgun. Specifically, as described next, you can put a significant amount of pressure on the trigger—eliminating most of the travel and poundage required to fire the weapon—prior to firing each shot. If this is done every time, any gun effectively has a light trigger pull. To accomplish this, manipulate the trigger as follows:

With the trigger actions on most semiautomatic pistols (except many DAOs), the initial travel consists of a relatively light amount of weight, generally called "take-up" or "slack," prior to actual sear disengagement. This initial travel may be slight or very pronounced. Press quickly through this part of the trigger pull, since it merely constitutes additional distance your finger must move and hence increases the chance you will jerk the gun off target.

With the take-up removed, you will next encounter a heavier section of the trigger action, the sear engagement that releases the hammer or striker and fires the weapon. Press through most of this section too, leaving only a fraction of the original pull weight remaining to be applied once the weapon pauses in a position that is sufficiently well-aligned with the target. You can interrupt or delay this final press should the weapon or target move out of alignment.

This combination of pressing out the take-up ("taking up the slack") and putting significant pressure on the trigger before committing to a shot is called "prepping" the trigger. If you are not already prepping your trigger before each shot, you will probably notice a dramatic improvement in your shooting once you begin doing it. With a double-action revolver or DAO auto pistol with a consistent pull weight throughout its entire travel, you should also get the trigger moving early. In this case there will be no discernable take-up, so just pull the trigger smoothly, the same speed all the way through, like zipping a zipper.

The question arises, "doesn't this create a risk of unintentional discharge?" It certainly does, especially when you are just learning to manipulate the trigger in this fashion. But any shot that occurs due to prepping the trigger a bit too aggressively should take place when the gun is pointed at (or at least toward) the intended target and the decision has been made to fire. In civilian scenarios, including police gunfights, the shooter will be facing an imminent lethal force threat at this time.

As long as you don't put your finger on the trigger until the decision to fire has been made, any discharge that occurs as a result of prepping the trigger will happen at one of two points in the threat engagement process: as either the first shot or the last. In both cases the discharge of the weapon will truly be a surprise and the shot will probably be a hit, provided the weapon is aligned with the target, as it should be at this point in the fight.

The more precise the shot in question, the more important prepping the trigger becomes. In reality, at 7 yards and under, you can pull any trigger smoothly through like a revolver and hit just fine, provided you isolate the trigger finger sufficiently. Hence the degree of precision required in trigger control will vary with the difficulty of the shot, just like the way your aim can change with the distance to the target or its size.

In all cases, the trigger finger must be the only part of the body that moves when the trigger is manipulated. In fact, ideally only the last two (distal) phalanges of this finger should move; the knuckle where the digit joins the hand should remain still. Isolating the trigger finger is partly a function of proper placement on the trigger, and thus of grip technique, but also a matter of practice. Creating the neural pathways required for reflexive execution of proper trigger control will

Bullet holes in the wood below the targets provides a permanent record of severe flinching by many shooters over several years of practice and qualification firing. (Andy Stanford)

require significant dry fire repetition, as described in Appendix B.

Good trigger control poses a challenge, particularly at speed and under stress, for a number of reasons. First of all, the faster you move your index finger, the harder it is to isolate from the other fingers. Try this experiment: with nothing in your hand, simulate pressing a trigger with your index finger while holding your other fingers and thumb still. Start slowly, then speed up. You will find that the quicker the index finger moves, the more difficult it is to keep the other digits from moving too.

Additionally, trigger control is at the mercy of several inherent human traits. Every person was born with only two fears; all the rest were learned. Unfortunately for the combat shooter, fear of loud noises is one of these. (The other is fear of falling.) Therefore, we have a natural instinct to flinch

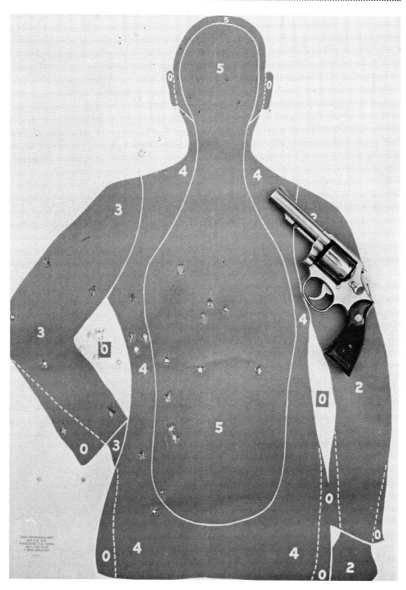

Most shots low and left: the result of a classic flinch in anticipation of blast and recoil for a right-handed shooter. This target was shot by an academy recruit during basic training. (Andy Stanford)

whenever a firearm discharges. This can be overcome with practice, but flinching in anticipation of the report and muzzle blast, along with bracing against recoil, results in more missed shots than any other cause, in my experience.

Speaking of recoil, humans also have a natural tendency to push back against something that pushes against them. The kick of a service-caliber handgun may be completely painless, but it can nonetheless elicit a counteracting response from the shooter. This, in turn, can easily shove the gun off target as the weapon is fired.

Common manifestations of these reactions to muzzle blast and recoil include "heeling" the gun—breaking the wrist with the hand pivoting upward, resulting in shots that strike high and/or toward the trigger hand side of the intended point of impact—and the classic body flinch, which pushes the shots low and/or to the opposite side. To shoot well, you must ignore the by-products of weapon discharge and cause the trigger finger to move in isolation.

For optimum performance, you must eliminate mental tension as much as possible. Keeping your mind calm is the goal. Trigger control is largely mental, and overcoming the above obstacles to textbook technique will depend on how well you can relax and accept recoil. Mental tension results in physical tension, which makes your trigger finger both slower and less sensitive. As discussed previously, relaxed shoulder muscles also yield benefits in recoil management.

Proper breathing will help you to relax. Target shooters fire during the natural respiratory pause after an exhale. The timing of the engagement will often preclude this premeditated approach to breath control, but nonetheless you'll want to keep your brain oxygenated. Toward this end, shouting commands at your adversary as appropriate (e.g., "No!" "Drop that weapon!" or "Contact right!") prevents you from holding your breath during a confrontation.

Under threat of bodily harm, you will likely experience yet one more aspect of human evolution that militates against good trigger control. Our autonomic nervous system reacts to a deadly threat with a myriad of changes to the body. One common result is a significant decrease in fine motor coordination, and in case you haven't figured this out by now, proper trigger manipulation is a fine motor skill.

As a shooter and an instructor, my number one marksmanship challenge is how to achieve good trigger control, in myself and my students, respectively. This is particularly true when shooting quickly under pressure. I have found no easy answer. Thousands of correct repetitions can help to make the desired motions a reflex, and live fire practice will desensitize you somewhat to the report and recoil of the weapon. Even so, you will undoubtedly find yourself striving for good trigger control every time you shoot.

7 FOLLOW-THROUGH

The subject of follow-through often gets short shrift when combat marksmanship is discussed. Most marksmanship instructors understand follow-through in the sense that the aim must be maintained for a fraction of a second after the sear releases the hammer or striker, allowing time for the projectile to exit the barrel. The follow-through required for surgical speed shooting is a more esoteric matter.

To shoot accurately at the maximum rate of fire, you must be ready to apply the final pressure to the trigger at the instant the sights settle back on the target. While the weapon is in recoil, the gun is out of action. Using this downtime to best advantage is the key. With sufficient practice, the following tasks can be accomplished while the muzzle is off target.

Two empty cases in the air and a third ejecting. Timing the reset-prep-fire cycle of the trigger with the recoil of the weapon is critical for accurate rapid fire. (Eleanor Stanford)

First of all, you must allow the trigger to travel forward until it resets (i.e., to the point at which you can pull the trigger again and fire the weapon). Different weapons have different reset characteristics. With some guns you barely have to release the trigger at all, while others require that the trigger be let most of the way forward. Note that optimizing your trigger reset to a particular weapon can be detrimental when firing a weapon with a significantly longer reset. In actuality, it is largely irrelevant how far the trigger finger travels during reset, even if it comes off the face of the trigger between shots. Additionally, resetting the trigger a specific distance is a fine motor skill that will inevitably degrade under stress.

Next, you must prep the trigger as described in the previous chapter. With practice you can reset and prep before the sights settle on target. If you prep the trigger heavily, as recommended with a street gun, the weapon should discharge multiple accurate rounds almost without conscious effort on your part, from the time the decision is made to fire until you choose to cease firing.

On a DAO auto pistol or DA revolver, stroke the trigger while the gun is in recoil but do not stage it per se. A DA trigger should stay in constant motion during the entirety of its rearward travel. Time your manipulation of the trigger to synchronize it with the motion of the pistol in recoil.

Whatever the action type of your gun, one key to accurate rapid fire is to keep the trigger busy. Instead of the traditional recipe of "aim then fire"—which often results in the shooter jerking the trigger in an attempt to take a "snapshot" of a good sight picture—correct the alignment of weapon and target while you are pressing/stroking the trigger.

A double-action auto that transitions to single action after the first shot poses a particular challenge, since the single action reset point is much different than the initial trigger position for the DA first shot. Mastering this type of weapon will generally require more practice than a gun with a consistent trigger pull.

As the weapon discharges, watch the front sight lift from the target, even if you aren't focused directly on the sight itself. The ability to describe where the sights were when the shot broke (i.e., "calling the shot") is a sign of an accomplished shooter. When you can do this consistently, you will be able to troubleshoot many marksmanship problems, identifying and then correcting your own errors.

Remember: the act of firing any given shot is not complete until the sights are back on target and the trigger prepped. You must practice until this reset-prep process occurs reflexively each time the weapon is fired. With such follow-through thoroughly ingrained, your finger will either be applying pressure to the trigger awaiting your brain to command it to fire, resetting the trigger, or it will be com-

When moving the weapon to another threat, first look to where you wish to direct the gun. (Clay Babcock)

pletely off the trigger, straight and raised as high as possible alongside the gun above the trigger guard to prevent an unintentional discharge.

Different pistols also have different recoil and cycling characteristics and will require different timing of the reset-prep-shoot process in all-out rapid fire. For instance, an M1911A1 .45 ACP with hardball loads has more muzzle flip than a Glock 19 9mm with defensive ammo, but the Glock has a sharper, if lighter, recoil than the .45. For maximum speed, you'll need to synchronize your trigger manipulation with the recoil of the weapon in question.

These recoil and cycling characteristics also play a major role in shot-to-shot split times between multiple targets, helping to move the gun to a new point of aim. In addition to resetting and prepping the trigger during recoil, you can use this time to transition the gun from target to target. With a stance that is neutral (as opposed to biased to one side), you can easily engage targets in either direction. With targets that are positioned very close together, the gun will actually seem to bounce between targets on its own. If you do everything right, the difference between two shots on one target and one round on each of two targets can be as little as 0.05 seconds. Splits on targets separated by a significant distance will be a bit longer, and you have to provide some additional impetus to move the gun to the new point of aim.

To shift from one target to the next, move your eyes to the intended point of aim as soon as the weapon discharges, then direct the gun there, pivoting at the knees, not the waist. Do not fire until the weapon pauses on target. Shooting when the gun is moving at speed can cause misses strung along the path of weapon travel. Track the sights in recoil, even when you aren't focused directly on them, and fire only when you see the sights pause on the spot you want to hit. This principle applies when engaging both single and multiple targets.

The concept of follow-through is important in a tactical sense as well. The protocol developed by tactics guru Lyle Wyatt provides good guidelines. After shooting, stay on target with the trigger prepped for a moment to help prevent you from dropping your guard too soon. Then, take your finger out of the trigger guard, lower the weapon to an appropriate ready position, and assess the situation to ensure that your adversary is really out of the fight. Next, scan a full 360 degrees for additional threats. Finally, top off your gun as described in Chapter 10, preparing to fight again if necessary. Movement to cover and post-incident verbalization (e.g., "Police. Call the Police," "Dispatch; shots fired," "Clear," etc.) should be incorporated into this protocol as appropriate.

CHAPTER

8

ONE-HANDED SHOOTING

A two-handed stance is certainly optimal from the standpoint of weapon stability, trigger control, and recoil management. However in the real world—as opposed to on the target range—situations often arise in which it is necessary or desirable to shoot with one hand. For instance, your support hand may be occupied opening a door or pushing a bystander out of the line of fire.

Additionally, there is significant evidence from actual shootings that many people will shoot one-handed under stress, even if they have been taught to shoot with both hands on the pistol. In particular, reacting to a close-range threat seems to elicit this response, especially if the shooter is moving or surprised. Yes, I know, one should not be "surprised at close range," but Murphy's law says stuff happens. In any event, the surprise that elicits one-handed shooting could be tactical, not strategic.

One-handed shooting takes two primary forms: visually verified fire from eye level and unsighted shooting at contact distance from a weapon retention position. These variations address different tactical situations and require completely different techniques. Let's start with eye-level shooting for situations beyond arm's reach. Naturally, all of the preceding discussion on aiming, trigger control, and follow-through still applies. Grip will be the same too, since it's impractical to have one grip for two-handed shooting and another when firing with one-hand unsupported.

As with two-handed shooting, lean forward to create an overbalance in the direction you are firing in order to counter recoil. When possible, you may wish to rotate your torso to put your weapon side forward. Ideal foot placement will therefore be gun side foot to the front. However, as noted previously, you often won't get to choose exactly where your feet will be during an actual fight.

To further minimize shot-to-shot recovery time, cant the top of your gun inward to the position where muscle tension is neutral. The gun will then come back to the original point of aim without additional effort on your part. You can find this point in practice by observing the path the front sight travels as the gun discharges, rotating your hand after every few shots until you locate the place where the gun returns on target after recoil. For most people this is between 15 and 45 degrees from vertical. A good starting place is the natural orientation of your hand when you point your index finger at something.

The same techniques apply when using your nondominant hand unsupported from eye level. Many people find it surprisingly easy to shoot slow fire with their "weak" hand, since they have not programmed any poor trigger control habits into the trigger finger on this side. Shooting from the

When firing with one hand unsupported, maximum results will be achieved with the pistol rotated to the point of neutral muscle tension, the firing side foot forward, and an aggressive forward lean. (Clay Babcock)

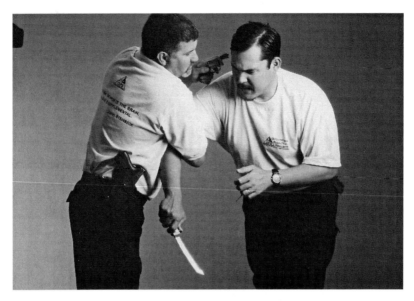

The ability to manipulate and fire using your left hand can be a useful skill in close-quarters combat. Here an empty hand knife defense is followed up with a backup gun. (Clay Babcock)

modern isosceles can actually enhance the ability to shoot with the nondominant hand unsupported, since both arms extend in a mirror image in the two-handed stance. (Weaver shooters sometimes fail to extend the nondominant arm sufficiently when using this hand only, perhaps because it is bent when they shoot with both hands.)

You may need to use your nondominant hand for any number of reasons, including injury to your dominant hand. Additionally, I've recently come to the conclusion that carrying a second pistol, accessible to both hands, as recommended by Louis Awerbuck, makes good sense. A backup gun is generally the fastest response to a weapon that malfunctions or runs out of ammunition. Also, knife defense and holstered weapon retention may preclude accessing your primary sidearm.

When shooting one handed from eye level, I like to place my nonshooting hand on the center of my chest. This keeps it in position to strike, block, or parry an incoming blow in a close-quarters confrontation. It's also a fairly natural place to cradle a wounded hand or forearm. In any event, you shouldn't let it dangle.

A contact-distance, weapon-retention position is the other staple one-handed technique that belongs in every combat handgunner's tactical toolbox. This category of shooting position probably does not receive the attention it deserves, especially given the likelihood of a contact-distance assault. So-called "hip shooting" has always been the recommend way to fire at extreme close range. From Ed McGivern to Rex Applegate to Bill Jordan, early combat handgunning gurus recognized the necessity of keeping the gun close to the body when in close proximity to an assailant.

Unfortunately, most hip shooting techniques do not take into account the violently physical nature of a close-quarters fight. This is clearly apparent in photos and diagrams that show the shooter's nonfiring hand hanging by his side, where it contributes nothing to defense or counterattack. Balance, too, receives little or no attention in many close-quarters shooting methods. In particular, the "Speed Rock" technique places the shooter significantly off balance backwards in order to raise the bullet point of impact to the upper chest. Given that even a perfect heart shot cannot physically produce instant incapacitation, you might as well target the pelvis and lower extremities at contact distance.

In my opinion, weapon-retention firing techniques should be thought of as hand-to-hand combat methods, not shooting stances. The primary goal in this case is *not* marksmanship but rather keeping your gun away from your assailant while creating an opportunity to disengage. My technique of choice for firing at bad breath range was developed in part by former Green Beret and fellow NTI shotist John Holschen. As a black belt martial artist with decades of

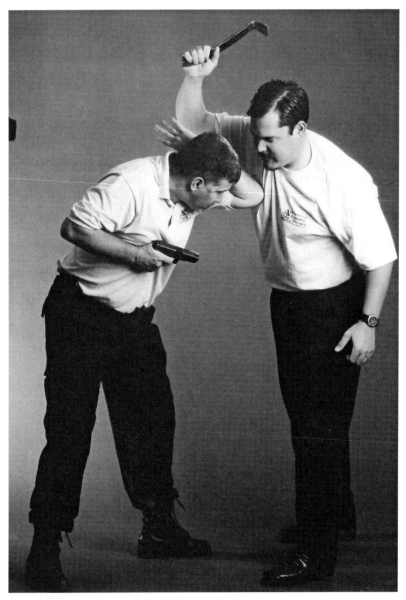

A close-quarters retention firing position is a staple part of any combat handgunning repertoire. (Clay Babcock)

experience, John clearly understands the unarmed fighting issues involved. His contact-distance shooting technique makes good use of the nonfiring arm and allows the shooter to remain balanced in the face of an aggressive opponent. To execute the technique in question, hold your gun hand wrist tight against the body, just under the pectoral muscle. You can exert much more strength from this position than with the gun hand near the belt line. Once the wrist comes off the body, the ability to prevent an assailant from taking the weapon is greatly diminished. Cant the weapon slightly outward to allow the hammer and/or slide to clear your body and clothing. (This is an interim position in the defensive draw stroke as described in Chapter 11.) Step forward off the line of attack and shift your weight forward aggressively as you raise your nondominant elbow in an upward arc, striking your assailant in the sternum or under the chin if possible. Depending on the relative position of you and your assailant, this can have a powerful impact in its own right and will often stop the forward momentum of a charging opponent. At the end of this motion, the nondominant arm should be tight against your head, covering against a blow.

The muzzle should point horizontal or somewhat lower when you are standing erect. Coupled with a forward lean, this will put your point of impact somewhere between the groin and the navel, allowing you the freedom to use your support hand against your assailant from his neck up. When you're justified in shooting and choose to do so, fire as fast as you can pull the trigger until you can break contact with your assailant and gain some distance. You can then finish the fight with visually verified gunfire if he continues to present a deadly threat.

Personally, I don't limit myself to the shield-block-cum-elbow-strike with the nondominant arm. As a defensive move, this only protects the high line and does not counter an edged weapon thrust to the midsection, a common assault among convicts and too serious a threat to ignore. Hence my

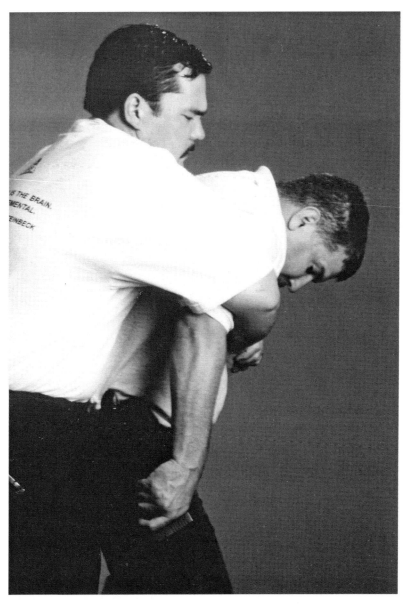

Above and next page: A contact-distance assault may require unorthodox firing techniques. (Clay Babcock)

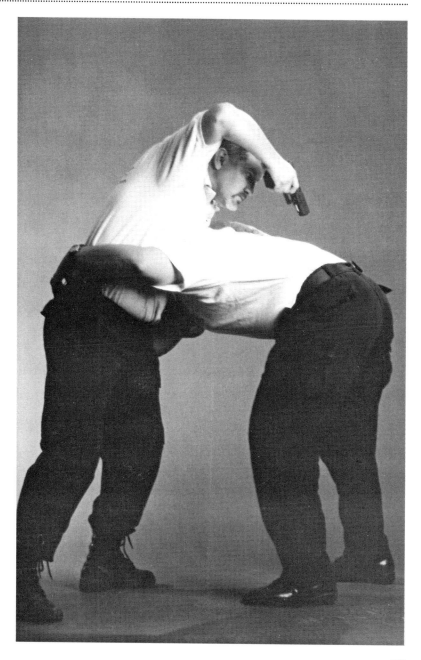

personal nondominant side arsenal also includes palm and forearm strikes to the head and neck as appropriate, plus parries, stop hits, and arm wraps for defense. Note, however, that in a contact-distance fight, it is very easy to sweep your free hand and/or arm with the muzzle of your weapon. The shield block technique does decrease the likelihood of shooting yourself in this manner and is a good general-purpose highline defense.

The aimed fire and weapon retention methods described in this chapter are just two of the more useful one-handed firing techniques. Other variations, some unconventional, may become necessary in a particular scenario. A tackle, rear bear hug, or knife attack may require you to adapt and improvise on the spot when using a handgun to overcome the assault at hand. So might groundfighting applications. In such situations it may help to think of your pistol as a lethal force lead injector. In reality, that's all it is anyway.

9 SHOOTING WHILE MOVING

Thunder Ranch Director Clint Smith popularized the doctrine of "shoot, move, communicate," which he borrowed from the U.S. military. The previous chapters have addressed the first of these actions. Now let's look at how to perform shooting techniques with your feet in motion.

Movement often plays a key role in your survival. In fact, you should usually be moving when not in a location where you are safe from gunfire. If you're not behind cover when the engagement begins, find some fast and get behind it at the first opportunity. A moving target is also harder to hit.

Shooting on the move is a common technique for today's tactical teams, both military and civilian. It can also be useful to the private citizen. When another's life is at stake, particularly a loved one, slow and deliberate movement may not be the answer. You may have to move out and take charge through speed, surprise, and violence of action.

Interestingly, this technique is not as new as you might believe. It traces its origins at least as far back as the "Mexican Defense Course," a staple pistol match in the old South West Pistol League. "The Mex" required firing while moving forward, backward, and laterally, engaging both single and multiple silhouette targets.

The key to shooting on the move is to use your legs as shock absorbers, minimizing bounce by isolating the upper body from the ground. To accomplish this, first bend your knees to lower your center of gravity. When moving forward, step in a rolling, heel-to-toe motion. Shorten your stride a bit and place your feet on or near a line in the direction you are moving. Walk straight ahead in the direction you are shooting; don't crab sideways. One advantage of the isosceles stance in this area is that it integrates better with your natural forward movement than the asymmetrical Weaver.

Moving backwards, widen your stance, as if walking on two railroad tracks. This will introduce some side-to-side sway, but it reduces the probability of tripping over your own feet. Even so, falling is a very real possibility when moving backwards quickly. Hence, you should learn to fall safely, and practice shooting from the ground.

You can also shoot while moving laterally, firing one- or two-handed as required by your natural body alignment. You can either shuffle sideways with the toes pointed in the direction of the target, like a soccer referee running the sidelines, or point your toes in the direction of travel, pivoting at the waist as necessary. When using the latter technique to move left to right as viewed from uprange, I shoot two-handed with my support (left) arm bent—this looks like a Weaver—and, traveling in the opposite direction, I fire with my dominant (right) hand unsupported. You can also fire one handed to the rear while moving almost directly away from the target.

The keys to accurate shooting while moving are to keep the knees bent so they act as a shock absorber for the upper body and to fire only when weapon alignment with the target is visually verified. (Eleanor Stanford)

Whatever your direction of travel, do not try and time your shots with your steps. Let the visually verified alignment of weapon and target determine when you fire. When shooting on the move, high-visibility, high-contrast sights such as the Ashley Express make this much easier. Note that your natural point of aim will often be degraded while moving, since your body position will be changing constantly, so the ability to point shoot from below eye level will suffer accordingly.

Though not technically shooting on the move, a slow and deliberate advance or retreat also warrants inclusion here. The technique used to accomplish this movement is the shuffle step (sometimes called a "step and drag"). Standing in your normal stance, the foot closest to the direction of travel steps out, widening the stance. Then the other foot moves, resuming your normal stance. When moving to the rear in this

Shooting while moving toward the firing hand side can be accomplished with a two-handed grip without sacrificing natural footwork. The resulting technique looks like a Weaver stance. (Clay Babcock)

When moving laterally toward the support hand side, firing one-handed will allow natural footwork. (Clay Babcock)

manner, feel for a clear path with your rearmost toe and keep your weight forward except as you move the front foot back. This will allow you to resist a charge. Whether moving forward or backward, the procedure is wide stance, then normal, *not* normal then narrow. This will allow you to shoot from a relatively balanced position at any point in the process.

Incorporate movement into all of your training, particularly that which involves presenting the weapon from the holster or tactical ready positions, reloading, malfunction clearances, and post-shooting procedures. These gun-handling tasks take you out of the fight temporarily, so develop the reflex of moving before and/or during the performance of such weapon manipulations. To do otherwise can program you to stand in one place when the lead is flying in your direction, a potentially fatal habit.

SECTION III
TACTICAL GUN HANDLING

Shooting quickly and accurately is only part of the skill-at-arms equation. You will also need to manipulate your gun safely and efficiently, get it on target in an expeditious manner, and keep it firing throughout the fight. These tasks comprise the elements of gun handling, and they are part of what separates the combat shooter from the mere marksman.

This section describes the best methods I've run across in my exposure to literally dozens of world class trainers. The techniques dovetail with the previously discussed shooting skills and follow the K.I.S.S (keep it simple, stupid) principle wherever possible. But before we proceed, let's quickly review firearms safety. Strict observance of the following rules is the sign of a true professional.

1. ALL GUNS ARE ALWAYS LOADED. Check the condition of any firearm immediately when you pick it up or it is handed to you, then always handle it in accordance with the other safety rules below.

2. NEVER LET YOUR MUZZLE COVER ANYTHING YOU ARE NOT WILLING TO DESTROY. Keep pistols holstered when not in use, and handle every firearm, loaded or not, as if there is a powerful laser beam emitting along the bore line that will vaporize everything it touches.

3. KEEP YOUR FINGER OFF THE TRIGGER UNLESS THE SIGHTS ARE ON THE TARGET. Except when you are in the act of firing, your trigger finger should be out of the trigger guard, pointed straight and angled up to its natural limit of motion. Make sure your finger is out of the trigger guard when drawing and reholstering.

4. BE SURE OF YOUR TARGET AND WHAT IS BEHIND IT. Do not shoot at silhouettes or sounds, have a safe backstop when practicing, and remember, *you* are responsible for the final resting place of every projectile you fire.

Additionally, always wear eye and ear protection when practicing, and don't handle firearms when you're under the influence of alcohol or other substances. Finally, it is your responsibility to keep your firearms secure from untrained and/or unauthorized individuals. If the gun is not within your immediate control (e.g., in the holster), lock it up. To do otherwise invites a preventable tragedy.

10 LOADING, UNLOADING, RELOADING, AND CLEARING MALFUNCTIONS

In a fight, it's critical that your gun goes "bang" each and every time you pull the trigger. Hence the number one attribute of any defensive firearm is reliability. But any mechanical device can malfunction, and guns hold a finite amount of ammunition. Hence, keeping your weapon in action throughout a fight may require that you reload it and/or clear stoppages.

We'll examine both of these critical gun-handling tasks in detail shortly, but first let's take a look at loading and unloading the weapon. With the specific procedures presented next, you'll perform—and therefore practice—the majority of the manipulations required to reload and clear malfunctions every time you load and unload your semiautomatic pistol. Revolver handling skills are treated separately at the end of the chapter. Three primary tasks address the majority of auto pistol handling: inserting the magazine so that it latches every time, cycling the slide by hand to eject/chamber a round, and locking the slide to the rear. Loading and reloading requires the first two of these tasks, immediate action malfunction clearance the second, and unloading the second and third. Remedial action malfunction clearance involves all three.

Botching any of these staple tasks can easily result in an operator-induced malfunction. Therefore you must not regard them lightly. Consistent, proper technique is the key to performance under pressure. Do it right each time in practice. Anything less is an incorrect repetition.

First of all, keep the auto pistol in your dominant hand at all times, maintaining a firing grip whenever possible. Not only will this facilitate the aforementioned weapon manipulations, it also puts you in the best possible position to respond to an immediate threat. Load, reload, and clear malfunctions with the pistol at approximately shoulder height, with your dominant side elbow close to the body. This provides an acceptable trade off between coordination, situational awareness, and "heads up" body language. The arm is also "cocked" to deliver a strike with the gun should this become necessary.

Don't extend the weapon unless it is ready to fire; holding a pistol at arm's length invites a takeaway attempt at the close quarters typical of many fights. You are also much less coordinated with the gun away from your body. Also, do not position the gun directly in front of your face unless you are aiming it. You cannot afford to obstruct your vision. Top competitive shooters keep the gun directly in front of their eyes, but they know where the targets are, and those targets can't kill them in any case.

Handle your magazines the same way every time in training, whether during administrative loading or high-stress

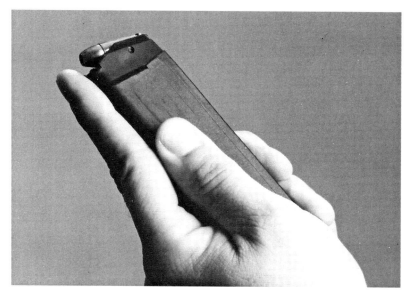

Always handle your magazines in a consistent manner, with the index finger along the front. (Clay Babcock)

exercises. Grasp the magazine in the nondominant hand with the index finger along the front and the base plate in the middle of your palm. This assists in both inserting the magazine into the well and seating it positively every time.

To insert the magazine, first orient the magazine well to correspond with the path the spare magazine will travel from the pouch when reloading. Next, index the flat at the back of the magazine with the corresponding flat at the back of the magazine well. Then roll the top of the magazine into the well. Lastly, when the magazine is aligned with the mag well, start it into the well and then seat it with one hard, positive motion. Shove the magazine home with the palm of the nondominant hand against the front of the magazine base plate. If you push at the rear of the base plate instead, the magazine hand may hit the gun hand or the weapon's frame at the back

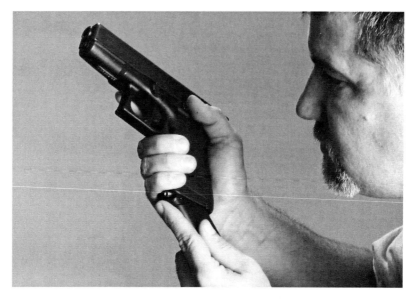

To insert a magazine, first index the flat at the back of the magazine with the flat at the back of the magazine well . . . (Clay Babcock)

of the mag well, preventing the magazine from seating fully and latching into the gun.

The above procedure works well under high stress with any service pistol. Resist the temptation to "thread the needle," i.e., attempting to insert and seat the magazine with one motion like IPSC shooters do. These competitors optimize their gun-handling techniques for match performance and install wide-mouthed mag well funnels on their pistols to maximize their margin for error. With many street guns, it's very easy to misalign the magazine and well at high speed under stress, with the end result of flinging the mag out of your hand.

With the magazine locked in place, you can then chamber a round by cycling the slide. Grasp the slide firmly at the rear on the cocking serrations. Right handers should use an over

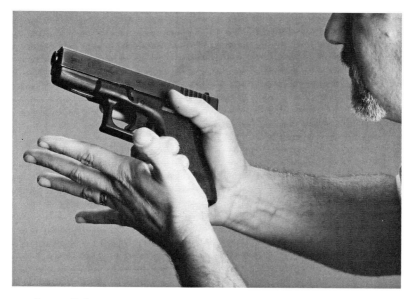

. . . then roll the magazine into the well and seat it hard with the palm of your hand against the front of the magazine floorplate. (Clay Babcock)

hand grip with the left hand; southpaws take a "slingshot" grip using the thumb and forefinger of the right hand. Make sure not to block the ejection port, especially with the over-hand method. Pull the slide fully to the rear, releasing it as the slide hits the frame at the end of its travel. As you pull the slide back, flip the gun smartly toward the right, rotating it clockwise approximately 90 degrees, ejection port down. This will let gravity assist in clearing the action when dealing with malfunctions, discussed below.

One common mistake is to ride your hand forward with the slide. Semiautomatic firearms were designed to cycle at high speed. Easing the slide forward can cause a failure to feed or to go fully into battery. Let it fly forward under the power of the recoil spring. At this point you can acquire a two-hand-ed grip on the weapon if appropriate for the tactical situation.

A right-handed person should pull the slide of an auto pistol to the rear using an overhand grip, rotating the weapon ejection port down. (Clay Babcock)

Weapons with ambidextrous decocker/safety levers like the Beretta 92 (M9) require caution when gripping the slide in order to prevent inadvertently moving the lever(s) to the down (decock/safety on) position. If you carry this type of pistol, experiment until you find a technique that works with the weapon in question.

When initially loading the pistol, you may wish to check the chamber to ensure the presence of a live round. In doing so, maintain a firing grip and pull the slide slightly to the rear by gripping the slide using a different method than the one you used to cycle it. In other words, if you loaded your gun with an overhand hold, perform your chamber check by easing the slide back slingshot fashion. This way your mind associates each type of grasp with a particular action: either pulling the slide fully to the rear or easing it back part way.

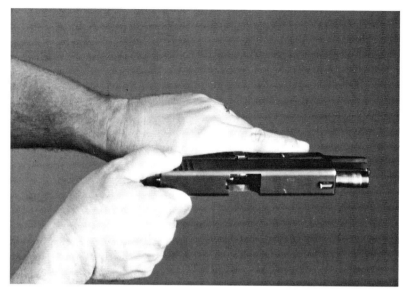

A left-handed person should pull an auto pistol slide to the rear using a slingshot grip while rotating the weapon ejection port down. (Clay Babcock)

With the action partially open, you can now insert a finger to feel for the chambered round. This tactile check can be performed without diverting your eyes from other tasks (e.g., looking for threats) and can also be done in the dark.

To unload a semiautomatic firearm, most people first remove the magazine, then clear the chamber. The procedure described next, advocated by fellow instructor Greg Hamilton, does double duty. It both clears the weapon for administrative purposes (i.e., when there is no immediate threat) and provides practice at the first half of the standard remedial action procedure, described shortly.

First, pull the slide to the rear and engage the slide stop lever, locking the action open. This will likely require that you shift the gun in your dominant hand in order to put your thumb in a position to push upward on the lever. Next,

Above: A right-handed person should perform a tactile chamber check by easing the slide partially to the rear with a slingshot grip, then feeling for the presence of a round in the chamber with his or her index finger. (Clay Babcock)

Right top: To unload a semiautomatic pistol, first lock the slide to the rear . . . (Clay Babcock)

Right bottom: . . . then remove the magazine and place it underneath the little finger of the firing hand. (Clay Babcock)

press the magazine release and use the nondominant hand to pull the magazine from the well. Then place the magazine under the little finger of your dominant hand, trapping it between the finger and the frame. Finally, cycle the slide several times to ensure that the chamber is clear.

With a reliable sidearm, shooting the gun empty is the most likely reason the weapon will quit firing in an actual confrontation. Counting your rounds during a fight is highly

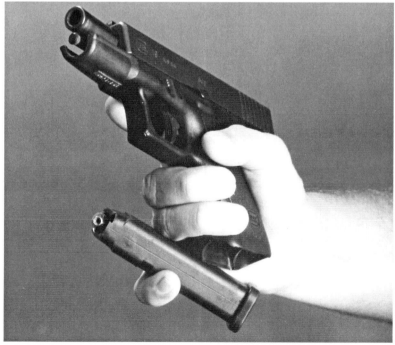

unlikely. Hence, the lightning fast, round-in-the-chamber IPSC speed load is better suited to carefully choreographed competition courses than the chaos of combat. As noted in Chapter 8, a second gun is often faster than a reload in the real world.

Reloading an empty gun requires exactly the same motions as those described previously for initially loading the weapon, with the additional steps of ejecting the empty magazine and pulling the spare from its pouch. Most of today's service pistols feature a frame-mounted magazine release button or lever accessible to the thumb and/or index finger, depending on model and whether you are right or left handed. You may have to shift your gun hand grip slightly to reach the magazine release; if so, you can reacquire a firing grip as you complete the reloading procedure.

Keep the magazine well oriented more or less vertically so gravity assists the magazine in falling free. Do not press the magazine release until you have confirmed that you have a spare mag available. If the empty magazine does not drop free, strip it from the weapon after you have pulled a loaded magazine from your pouch. Then orient the gun to accept the fresh magazine and seat it as described previously.

Immediately after you've seated the new magazine, pull the slide to the rear and release it to chamber a new round. This is a gross motor skill compared with pressing down on a small slide stop lever. It works better under stress and when you're wearing gloves. Also, you practice this action each time you load your pistol. Lastly, this procedure results in a chambered round even when the slide stop has failed to hold the slide to the rear after the last round was fired and the chamber is empty. Of course, this also recharges a weapon that still has ammunition in the magazine and/or chamber. The only penalty you pay is ejecting the round initially up the spout. For simplicity's sake, I suggest using the above method for both situations (i.e., slide forward or locked to the rear). Then the only other reload technique you'll need to learn is the tactical (aka magazine-save) reload.

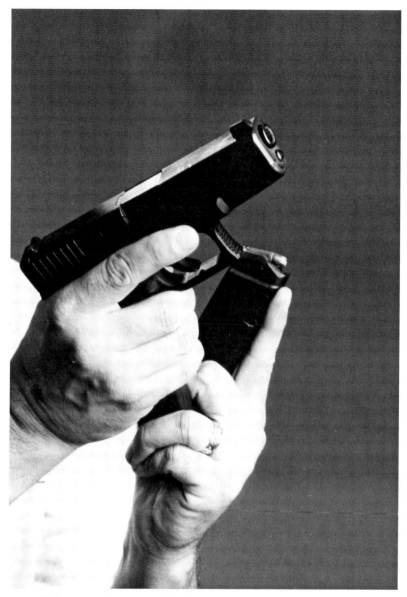

A tactical or magazine-save reload requires that the shooter retain the partially expended magazine that was in the weapon initially. (Clay Babcock)

The "tac load" is performed during a lull in the action, or when the fight appears to be over. The goal of this procedure is to top off the gun while retaining any ammunition remaining in the magazine. Most people use some variation of the following steps.

After withdrawing the spare magazine from the pouch, bring the nondominant hand close to the butt of the weapon. Then press the magazine release, dropping the mag in the gun partially out of the gun, and stop it with the nondominant palm. Next, use two fingers of the nondominant hand to pull the magazine from the gun, whichever two fingers work best for you. (I use my middle and ring fingers.) Finally, while retaining the partially depleted magazine between your fingers, insert and seat the full magazine. The partially depleted magazine can then be stowed for future use. If you carry just one spare, stick the partial mag back in your pouch, where you are used to obtaining reserve ammo. With two or more spares, put the partial in your pocket so you don't confuse it with a fully loaded one.

Some instructors recommend performing a chamber check after a tac load. In my opinion, attempting this fine motor skill invites an operator-induced double feed. Remember, at this moment in time you've just been fighting for your life and may be a bit shaky. Instead of easing the slide back, simply cycle the action hard. This gross motor skill will ensure that there is a round in the chamber, provided you seated the magazine. (It's a good idea to tug on the mag to confirm this.) Yes, you'll most likely eject a round when you do this (unless the slide is closed on an empty chamber), but it's a small price to pay for ensuring there's a round in the chamber.

Truth be told, the tac load is a complex motor skill requiring significant practice to perfect. An acceptable alternative is to simply perform an empty load, then pick up the partial magazine if there is time. Kneeling before you press the magazine release will facilitate this, provided it is tactically sound to do so.

The above reload and unloading procedures all entail ejecting a live round on the ground unless the chamber happens to be empty. Do not look at where this round goes or you'll develop the habit of "cycle the slide, look at the ground." If you can keep from even thinking about that round, so much the better. Remember: we're training for combat. The cost of a cartridge or even a whole box of them is miniscule compared with your life.

If your handgun quits firing for any reason during a fight, including running dry, the quickest way back into action is almost always a second gun, provided you always carry a backup piece and you always practice drawing it in response to the appropriate stimuli. However, the fact is that many people carry only one weapon, and in any case it's still important to understand how to get your sidearm firing again post haste in an emergency.

As with reloading, procedures for clearing common weapon malfunctions employ the skills required for loading and unloading. Auto pistol stoppages can occur for many reasons: failure to feed, extract, eject, or go fully into battery; an unseated magazine; and a double feed. The latter two are generally a result of operator error. A dirty gun can contribute to these problems, and parts breakage can also put you out of commission, often until the gun can be repaired. Hence frequent cleaning and proper maintenance are a must.

Each kind of malfunction can be cleared with a type-specific action, optimized for that particular stoppage. However, this requires that the problem first be diagnosed, which in turn takes time and forces you to take attention away from the fight. Additionally, identifying the type of stoppage becomes problematic in low light and darkness. The following default procedures will clear most malfunctions aside from those caused by a broken part.

Whenever you pull the trigger and the gun does not fire, your first priority is to move if possible. As you do this, tap the magazine upward to ensure that it is fully seated and rack the slide, flipping the pistol ejection port down. (Sound familiar?) Re-engage the threat as necessary. This used to be taught as "tap, rack, bang," but then someone figured out that the situation might de-escalate during the malfunction clearance, making gunfire unnecessary and hence excessive force.

If a "tap, rack, re-engage" does not solve your problem— i.e., if you pull the trigger again and the gun doesn't fire— proceed with remedial action as follows. Again, your first priority is to move; remedial action takes much longer than immediate action, so get to cover or disengage if possible.

Lock the slide to the rear. Rip the magazine from the well and place it under the little finger of your dominant hand, as when unloading the weapon. Work the action several times to ensure a clear chamber, pulling it fully to the rear and releasing it just like you do when loading or reloading. Then reload the weapon as described previously. ("Lock, rip, work, reload.") Some pistols don't require that the slide be locked back before removing the magazine, but the procedure described will work with all pistols.

You can either retrieve the magazine that was initially in the weapon from under your dominant hand little finger or use a fully loaded spare if the original one is depleted, damaged, or otherwise suspect. If you choose the latter, you can let the original magazine fall to the ground as you pull the new one from the pouch. Just don't abandon the partially depleted magazine until you confirm that you have another available.

Note that if you've totally ingrained these habits to the level of unconscious competence, you will likely respond to running out of ammunition with immediate action, i.e., "tap, rack." If you recognize that your gun is empty at this point, you'll reload then. Otherwise, you'll probably attempt to fire again, then proceed with remedial action when the gun doesn't discharge, ending up with a loaded gun regardless. While slower than responses optimized to each contingency, this set of actions will keep your gun in the fight without requiring that you deliberate about what to do.

If you carry a wheelgun, you'll need to accomplish the same objectives, but using a different set of subtasks. To load, first, press the cylinder latch, then immediately shift the weapon to your nondominant hand as you open the cylinder. This will let you use your more coordinated hand for manipulating speed-loading devices or single rounds of ammunition. Keep the cylinder from rotating by sticking the middle and ring fingers (right handers) or thumb (southpaws) through the cylinder cutout in the frame.

Immediately upon securing the weapon in your nondominant hand, orient the gun muzzle up and smack the ejector rod smartly with your dominant palm. This will give you practice at the initial step in a speed load. Some people use the nondominant hand thumb to push the ejector rod as they reach for ammunition with the other hand, but this is not as positive as smacking it. This will also help prevent an empty case from getting stuck under the ejector star. These initial steps of quickly opening the cylinder, shifting the weapon to the other hand, and ejecting spent rounds are key revolver skills.

Next, tip the weapon muzzle down, then insert single rounds or a cylinder full of ammo. When using a speed-loader, align two rounds and the rest will follow. Let go of the speedloader after releasing the cartridges; if you hold onto it, you may pull rounds back out of the chambers. Likewise if you let the muzzle tip up during this process, rounds may fall out due to gravity. Resume your dominant hand grip as you close the cylinder.

A revolver tac load requires removing the spent casings while retaining the live rounds in the cylinder. To do this, open the cylinder and shift the gun into the nondominant hand as usual. With the muzzle pointed down, ease the ejector rod back partway with your nondominant side thumb (right handers) or index finger (lefties) instead of smacking it. With service ammo, the empties should protrude when the ejector rod is released due to case wall expansion. The unfired rounds will slide back into their chambers. You can then pick

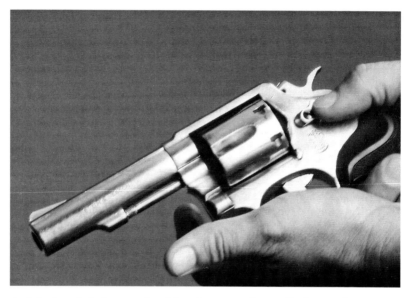

A right-handed shooter should swing a revolver cylinder out by activating the cylinder thumb latch with the right thumb, pressing the cylinder with the left hand middle and ring fingers, and transferring the weapon to the left hand for loading and unloading. (Clay Babcock)

the hulls out of the chambers and replace them with live rounds. You'll also want to be completely familiar with the direction the cylinder turns in the event you have to partially load the weapon. Colts turn clockwise; S&Ws and Rugers, counterclockwise.

For years, revolvers had a reputation for reliability that far exceeded that of any auto pistol. Today's autos fare much better in this regard, but wheelguns still generally give you "six for sure" (or five, or seven, or whatever). With a clean and well-maintained weapon, revolver malfunctions are usually ammunition related. Common problems include high primers, plus bullets that move forward out of the shell casing due to recoil. Both can tie up the cylinder. Confirming that the cylinder spins

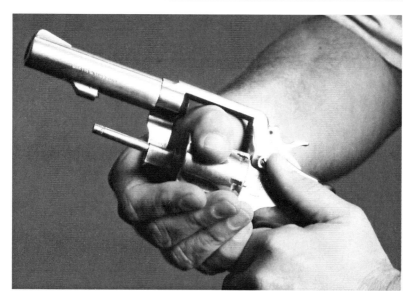

A left hander should press the thumb latch with the left thumb, swing out the cylinder with the right thumb, and transfer the weapon to the right hand for loading and reloading. (Clay Babcock)

freely after initially loading the gun will avoid the first problem; properly crimped ammunition is the solution to the second.

In the event of an injury, you may have to operate your weapon with one hand. You can cycle the slide of a semiauto by hooking the rear sight on your belt, pocket, or shoe. Alternately, you can kneel and wedge the slide behind your knee. With a little practice you can open the cylinder and push the ejector rod of a revolver with one hand. You can then shove the gun into your waistband or back in the holster to load. Where there's a will, there's a way, so don't give up. Adapt, improvise, and overcome.

The above is just one approach to gun handling, optimized for use under extreme stress. In reality the goal is to

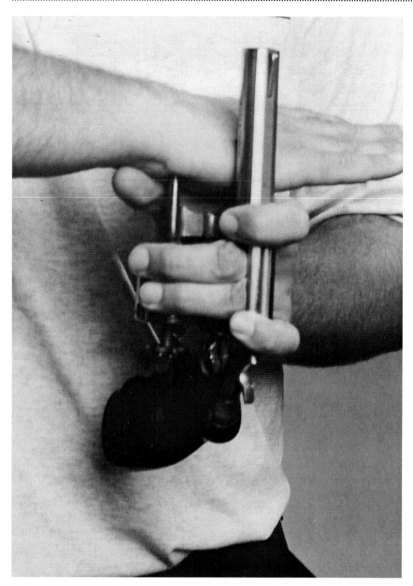

With the muzzle pointed up, smack the ejector rod with your dominant hand palm to maximize the probability that all empty casings will fall free. (Clay Babcock)

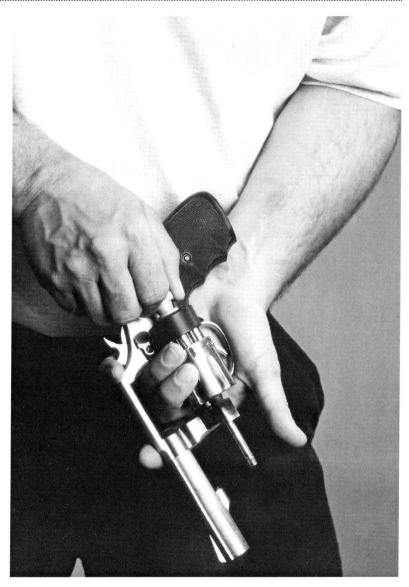

The muzzle should be pointed down when loading a revolver so the cartridges will fall into the chambers due to gravity. (Clay Babcock)

keep the gun running, and as long as you accomplish this in an expeditious fashion, the particulars are secondary. That said, don't overestimate your ability to perform complex motor skills when someone is trying to kill you. In an actual gunfight, fingers can turn quickly to flippers, so adhering to the K.I.S.S. principle is generally a good idea. Whenever possible, you should move while performing any of these weapon manipulations in the open, assuming cover if available and appropriate to your proximity to the assailant. Don't just stand flat-footed, fiddling with the weapon. Whether you are reloading or clearing a malfunction, your weapon is temporarily out of commission. If you don't carry a backup weapon, in a worst case scenario—out of ammunition or hopelessly jammed gun—you will either have to continue the fight with makeshift tools (e.g., using your pistol as an ersatz impact weapon), bluff with a nonfunctional firearm, or run away.

11 THE DEFENSIVE DRAW STROKE

As noted in the first chapter, handguns are relatively underpowered and difficult to shoot well under stress compared with a rifle, shotgun, or submachine gun. On the plus side, they offer concealability, portability, effective employment with one hand, and the ability to hold the weapon close while maneuvering in tight quarters.

You can don a pistol in the morning and it will remain close at hand throughout the day, without conscious effort on your part. A holster makes this possible. Clearly then, you'll need the ability to draw your weapon quickly and consistently. The following draw stroke accomplishes this and facilitates a response to both contact-distance threats and those at longer range.

First, the dominant hand moves to the pistol, coming down on it from the top. Immediately establish a firing grip and disengage any retention device(s) such as a thumb break. With a police duty rig with additional retention features (e.g., the Safariland SSIII), any required rocking or twisting of the gun also occurs at this point.

Moving laterally off the line of attack is also strongly recommended. This footwork is performed simultaneously with the first step of the draw stroke. You can literally dodge a bullet with this movement, since action beats reaction.

If a concealment garment is worn, clear it as the dominant hand moves to the pistol. With an unbuttoned coat, jacket, or shirt, claw the garment back with all fingers on the dominant hand. With a sweatshirt, buttoned shirt, or similar attire, pull it high with both hands, initially grabbing the bottom of the shirt as near the holster as possible.

As the garment is cleared and the weapon is gripped, move the support hand to the chest, palm heel against the body, thumb pointed up along the centerline of the body, index finger at or just below the dominant side nipple. This puts the support hand in position to assume a two-handed grip on the weapon and stages it to execute hand-to-hand combat techniques.

In a contact-distance situation, the nondominant arm should immediately perform the shield-block-cum-elbow-strike described previously. The shield block also clears the nondominant arm from the path of the muzzle when you're wearing a shoulder holster. Alternately, the nondominant hand can hit your assailant at the neck or above with some other hand/arm blow, or parry a gun grab attempt or edged weapon attack. In fact, in response to a sudden assault, the support hand may perform one of these actions in lieu of moving to the center of the chest at all.

In any case, as both hands move and you step off the attack line, lean forward to shift your weight toward your opponent. Doing so now both puts you in your final body posture as early as possible and braces you against a charging assailant. Remember, you are drawing your weapon in response to a deadly force threat, very likely at close range. Next pull the gun straight up out of the holster to the body's natural limit of travel. As the weapon clears the holster, rotate the muzzle forward, putting the hand, wrist, and arm in their final alignment. The dominant side elbow should stay close to the body; avoid letting it "chicken wing" to the side where it could be used as a lever by an assailant at contact distance. Additionally, keeping the elbow in tight contributes to the desired outward cant.

The dominant hand and pistol are now in the previously described weapon-retention position. When dealing with an assailant at contact distance, you may elect to remain in this position until you can create distance. Depending on the circumstances, you can shoot, use the gun as an impact weapon, or reholster. A close-range confrontation may require any of these actions, so remain flexible.

These initial movements should be performed as quickly as possible. Move without unnecessary muscle tension, snapping loosely into position as if jolted by electricity. Accelerate from 0 to 60 like a race car in the red. In addition to stepping off the line between you and your assailant, as mentioned above, you may continue moving to cover or to enfilade multiple opponents.

If your assailant is beyond arm's length, move the gun away from your body and toward the target. The support hand joins the dominant hand close to the body, establishing a final firing grip. Alternately, extend the gun with one hand unsupported. In either case, the muzzle of the gun should track vertically up the assailant's centerline; swinging in from an angle is much harder to control.

The bore line should remain pointed in the direction of the target, with the barrel slightly elevated, as the weapon is raised. The sooner you move the pistol to your sight line, the sooner you can start using the sights to refine and/or

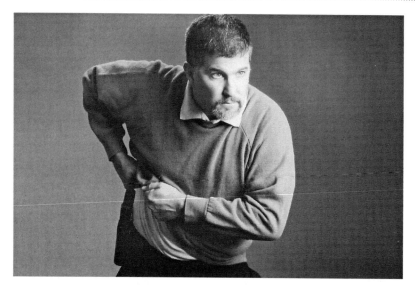

When drawing a concealed pistol, clear any covering garments prior to establishing a grip on the holstered weapon. (Clay Babcock)

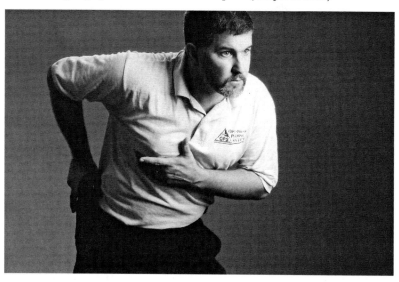

Grip the weapon and release all retention devices, simultaneously stepping off the line of attack if possible. (Clay Babcock)

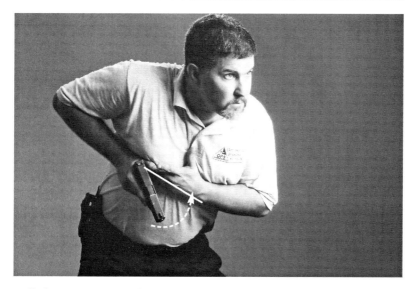

Pull the weapon out of the holster, rotating the muzzle up to retention position. (Clay Babcock)

Establish a two-handed firing grip on the weapon. (Clay Babcock)

Raise the gun to eye level and begin visual verification of weapon alignment and trigger manipulation. (Clay Babcock)

Extend the weapon fully, firing as it comes to a stop if appropriate. (Clay Babcock)

confirm weapon alignment. Therefore, bring the weapon up to the sight line from retention position, then out toward the target rather than out then up. You can establish initial alignment with your front sight on the intended point of impact, then fire as soon as the rear sight rises into position as the arms extend.

Classic draw stroke errors include "bowling"—i.e., arcing the pistol down, under, and up—and "cowboying," with the muzzle travelling up and over the sight line, like a rainbow. The latter is also known as the "Zebco draw" (after the fishing rod and reel advertised on TV by that company). Have a qualified person observe your draw stroke to catch these errors. Also make sure that the muzzle does not sweep any part of your body, both while drawing and while reholstering. This is especially important when drawing from a seated position, as when in a vehicle or at a table.

As you bring the gun to bear, decelerate smoothly, 60 to 0, like an unexpected stop by a limo driver who doesn't want the boss to spill coffee on his lap. If you continue at full speed to the end of your draw stroke, the gun will come to a jarring halt. This will produce unwanted vibrations, analogous to a tuning fork, that will require you to wait before you shoot. Place the gun lightly on target. You want to achieve your natural speed, as when you reach for a light switch or point in response to a request for directions.

A couple of visualization tricks may help you in stopping the gun precisely at the desired position in space. First, think of *pulling* the gun forward to the desired spot with your fingers rather than pushing it with the palms of your hands. This will often result in more awareness of the direction in which the muzzle is pointed as well as better control of its movement and orientation. Second, mentally project the front sight onto the target as you bring the weapon to bear. It would be easy to hit the target if the front sight were actually on the target, right? Imagining it there accomplishes much the same thing in your mind.

For the quickest possible draw—defined as fire stimulus to the moment your gun discharges—the trigger should be prepped as you extend your arms. Apply the final pressure to the trigger just as the gun comes to a complete halt, verifying weapon alignment via the sights or other feedback as the gun comes to a stop. Then reset and prep the trigger for the next round.

The above technique should be performed as one smooth motion in combat, but you should break the draw stroke down into steps when first learning it. Start from full extension and then work backwards one step at a time, to the two-handed close-quarters ready position described in the next chapter, then to the point that the hands separate from the pistol, and ultimately to the holster. This way you will always move through a familiar reference point to previously practiced movements, which in turn were initially derived from correct weapon alignment.

When you're finished shooting—and have assessed the condition of known assailants, scanned for additional threats, topped off your gun, and moved to cover as appropriate—you may wish to reholster. To do so, simply reverse the above draw stroke. First bring the weapon back to your chest. Leave your nondominant hand on your chest as you pull the gun into a retention position; this will prevent you from muzzle sweeping it.

If you fire from a low shooting position, e.g., kneeling, and it's appropriate to the tactical situation, stand before you put the gun back in the holster. This will help to prevent you from pointing the gun at your legs. Perform one last 360 degree threat scan, then reholster and refasten any retention devices. By stepping backwards through the draw procedure, you again pass familiar reference points, assisting you in reholstering by feel.

To recap, the defensive draw stroke occurs in two phases: acceleration and deceleration. Establish a grip on the weapon and withdraw it from the holster at maximum speed into a weapon retention position. Move laterally relative to your assailant as you do this. The support hand comes to the center of the chest or executes a shield block, parry, etc., during this phase. Then extend the weapon, assuming a firing grip and progressively slowing down, stopping as the gun reaches its final position aligned with the target, working the trigger on the way out. You can stop this process halfway to deal with a contact-distance threat.

You'll need to modify the above procedure for use with shoulder holsters, fanny packs, ankle rigs, etc. For instance, with a shoulder holster, your nondominant hand can execute a shield block as the initial move to clear it from the line of the muzzle during the draw. Also, be sure that your technique allows execution of the draw stroke with one hand only if necessary (e.g., opening the flap on a fanny pack with your gun hand, in case the support hand is otherwise occupied).

And remember, a quick draw is no substitute for good awareness skills. Don't depend on a fast presentation from the holster to get you out of trouble. If you see an imminent assault in time and cannot safely effect a escape, the techniques described in the next chapter can provide you with a significant edge.

CHAPTER

12

TACTICAL
READY
POSITIONS

While the ability to quickly present your handgun from the holster is undeniably a valuable skill, the quickest possible draw is to have gun in hand before the shooting starts. With a firing grip on the weapon, you eliminate the variables that can result in a botched presentation, and you can get the gun on target that much more quickly. The ready positions described in this chapter provide a number of tactically sound alternatives to a variety of situations.

Gunsite traditionally taught the muzzle depressed ready position, also known as low ready or the guard position, for use with the Weaver stance. It is simply the normal firing stance with the muzzle pointed down at approximately 45 degrees.

Rex Applegate taught a one-handed version of the same ready position in his point shooting system. This approach has a few major drawbacks for general purpose use. First, the weapon protrudes excessively from the body, inviting and facilitating a take away attempt by an adversary at close quarters. Secondly, with the arms extended, fatigue can set in during an extended search, with the gun pointing increasingly downward with the passing of time. Alternately, some shooters tend to let their guns creep up toward their lines of sight under stress, obscuring the lower part of their fields of view.

For these reasons, I recommend a close-quarters ready position instead, with the weapon held close to the chest. Bring the weapon to the midline of the body, with the bore approximately at nipple height. Depending on the situation, the muzzle can be oriented toward the threat, up, down, or toward the nondominant side. In all cases, your trigger finger should be straight and raised to its natural limit of travel unless you are shooting. Not only is the weapon less accessible to an assailant at arm's length, if someone does grab for it, you can exert greater strength from this position than with the weapon extended, as noted previously. You can quickly bring the firearm back along your side for weapon retention or even fire from this position if necessary. Since the weapon is on your body centerline, the natural tendency to face a threat squarely will provide coarse weapon alignment with your adversary's centerline at close range.

On the down side, this close-quarters ready position does not project aggressive intent to the degree that pointing the weapon with extended arms does. In fact, as surprising as it may seem, in some instances the person you're challenging may not even see your gun. Do not discount body language as a significant factor in dominating a situation! Additionally, even with the muzzle pointed toward the threat, close-quarters ready is slightly slower from fire stimulus to eye-level weapon discharge than an extended low ready, a difference of approximately 0.15 to 0.20 seconds in my testing.

A close-quarters ready position facilitates a quick first shot while keeping the weapon back to minimize the possibility of a disarm. (Clay Babcock)

If distance between combatants allows, extending the weapon when challenging an assailant projects an aggressive body language and also decreases time to first shot. (Clay Babcock)

Thus, when confronting a potential or manifest assailant who warrants having a gun pointed at him—and assuming enough distance to do so without undue risk of a disarming attempt—consider extending your arms and aiming the weapon no higher than an opponent's pelvis or hip socket. From this position, you can see the assailant's hands. Should he present a lethal threat, you can either fire immediately or track up his centerline to another target. Additionally, with a male adversary it will appear that you are aiming at his genitals, particularly if your firearm is equipped with a visible laser. (Relatively few violent criminals are female, though they do exist.)

When working in close proximity with others, you can easily muzzle sweep your partner(s) with the close-quarters ready position. Yes, you can tip the muzzle down to divert the weapon while maintaining your normal firing grip, but this requires muscle tension and conscious thought to maintain. Fatigue can quickly set in, and if your attention is drawn elsewhere, the muzzle will naturally point horizontal. Instead, I suggest breaking your firing grip altogether and assuming position "sul" (Portuguese for "south"), developed by former Force Recon Marine Max Joseph while he was conducting training in Brazil.

Position sul points the muzzle straight down. The tips of your two thumbs index against each other, and your dominant hand middle finger indexes against the nondominant index finger. You can quickly shift to close-quarters ready as the situation permits—for example, when you become the person on point in a team tactics situation—or bring the weapon to eye level to fire as necessary. In a dynamic situation, sul provides maximum margin for error, allowing you to move very close to other people without pointing your gun at them. From a safety standpoint it's the next best thing to a holstered pistol, provided the muzzle is pointed straight down.

In many situations, position sul may be preferable to the close-quarters ready position, since with the latter there is an increased risk of shooting a bystander if startled. Likewise, when there is insufficient justification to point the weapon directly at your opponent, the extended "challenge" position can be used while aiming at the ground in front of him. This sacrifices very little in the way of response time, and with proper demeanor and verbalization, the effect is still very intimidating. As good guys, we must err on the side of caution, shooting only those who pose an actual threat.

Obviously, these three are not the only ready positions ever developed. A few instructors still promote "high ready," with the muzzle pointed upward. Though most trainers eschew high ready, it has its pros and cons just like any other technique. The Los Angeles Police Department teaches officers to point the gun straight down at the ground, with arms

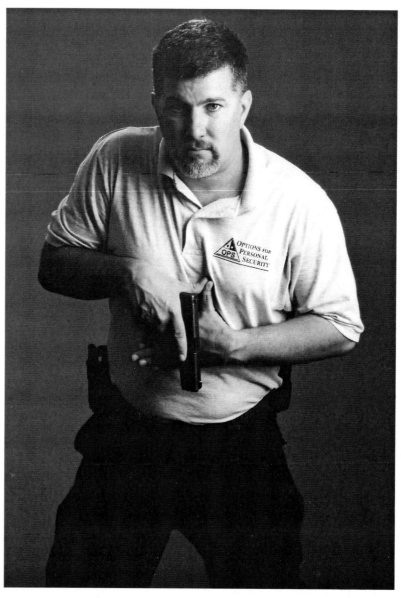

Position "sul" is the next best thing to a holstered weapon when working in close proximity to team members or bystanders. (Clay Babcock)

extended, when working around others; this is safe enough, but is not as well-suited to close-quarters scenarios as position sul. In some situations, particularly with pocket pistols and small revolvers, you can also assume a concealed ready, preserving the element of surprise. Modify techniques as necessary, using the preceding information as you see fit.

CONCLUSION

Let's recap the most important points from each chapter. Surgical shooting at the maximum possible speed provides the best odds of quickly stopping a determined assailant. The elements of the modern isosceles—a specific grip and stance—facilitate this type of combat marksmanship better than the Weaver stance. A traditional sight picture will often be too slow for close defensive shooting and unnecessary in many cases. Prepping the trigger greatly enhances trigger control, as does a reflexive reset during rapid fire.

One-handed shooting is a critical skill, using both eye-level fire and close-quarters retention techniques. So is shooting on the move, isolating the upper body with the legs.

Performed properly, loading and unloading the pistol can provide repetition of the bulk of manipulations required for reloading and nondiagnostic malfunction clearance. And gun-handling skills should also include well-practiced tactical ready positions, plus a draw stroke that moves through the aforementioned close-quarters position.

In a fight, the techniques covered in this book must be reflexive. Otherwise, you won't perform them well, if at all, under duress. The resources and practice drills in the appendices should assist you in becoming "unconsciously competent." However, they are not intended as a substitute for training under the watchful eye of a qualified instructor, one who can provide the feedback and personal coaching necessary to ensure proper technique.

In a violent confrontation, prowess at surgical speed shooting and tactical gun-handling techniques can contribute to your survival. But bear in mind that skill at arms is just one factor in the outcome of a such an encounter, and it is not usually the most important. Mind-set and tactics generally achieve more in the big picture. And always remember: your number one option for personal security is a commitment to avoidance, deterrence, and de-escalation.

Good luck, and stay as safe as your situation allows.

A RESOURCES

TRAINING BY AUTHOR

Options for Personal Security, P.O. Box 489, Sebring, FL 33871-0489, www.optionsforpersonalsecurity.com

BOOKS AND VIDEOS

Shooting From Within by J. Michael Plaxco. Perhaps the best book for the average shooter on competitive shooting technique. Approximately half of the chapters pertain to matters of interest to the hard-core defensive or tactical shooter. Available from Zediker Publishing, P.O. Box 1497, Oxford, MS, 38655, www.zediker.com.

Practical Shooting: Beyond Fundamentals by Brian Enos. More ethereal than Plaxco's book, this nonetheless useful text could have been titled "Zen in the Art of Practical Pistolcraft." It is most suitable to those who already have a significant amount of shooting experience. Also available from Zediker Publishing.

Jim Grover's Defensive Shooting Series. A former member of the U.S. military special operations community, Mr. "Grover" covers not only the modern isoceles as a combat stance but many esoteric gun handling and tactical methods as well. Four videos, available from Paladin Press.

Secrets of a Professional Shooter by Ron Avery. A videotape version of Avery's skills development course, covering the major aspects of the modern isoceles and related technique. To order, contact The Practical Shooting Academy, P.O. Box 630, Olathe, CO, 81465, www.practicalshootingacad.com.

Bullseyes Don't Shoot Back. The book the late Col. Rex Applegate co-authored with Mike Janich thoroughly documents classic point shooting doctrine. Published and sold by Paladin Press.

Fighting with Firearms and *Advanced Fighting with Firearms* (videocassettes) by Andy Stanford. My two Paladin Press tapes cover a number of important topics beyond the scope of this book.

SIGHTS
AO Sights
2401 Ludelle St.
Ft. Worth, TX 76105
www.aosights.com

TARGETS
Mountain Pass Option Target
Cumberland Tactics
P.O. Box 1400
Goodlettsville, TN. 37070
www.guntactics.com

APPENDIX

B TRAINING DRILLS

An Indonesian martial arts adage states, "Repetition is the mother of skill." This is certainly true, but remember: only perfect practice makes perfect. Pay attention to detail during all of your training sessions.

Dry practice with an empty weapon provides some of the best training around. Not only will you get plenty of reflex-building repetition, dry firing allows you to develop trigger manipulation skills without flinch-inducing noise and recoil. Be sure to simulate trigger reset with each trigger press.

Dry fire safety is critical. Unload your gun in a room different than the one in which you will be dry firing, and leave the ammunition there. Triple check that your weapon is empty before proceeding. Point the weapon in a safe direction, preferably one that will stop bullets. If you are interrupted for any reason, check the gun again. When you are finished, say to yourself, aloud, "I am done dry firing." Many people have put holes in property or worse due to one last "dry fire" after they recharged their weapon.

If you fired from the Weaver stance in the past, it will take at least a month of daily dry fire practice before you begin to feel comfortable with the modern isosceles. I know; I went through the same retraining process myself. In the beginning, the isosceles felt totally unnatural. In the end, however, it became abundantly clear that it was the contorted Weaver that was out of sync with the human body.

Obtain some dummy rounds so you can practice all of your shooting and gun-handling tasks, including reloading and malfunction clearances. To develop your draw stroke, work backwards from full extension. This way you will always move into a familiar position. First move from close-quarter ready to the full isosceles. Then back up one step to retention ready, with your nondominant hand on your chest. Next, start with your dominant hand on the holstered pistol. Finally execute the entire draw from a variety of initial hand positions.

Moving on to live fire drills, begin by shooting at small dots from relatively close range. This reinforces the fundamentals without requiring targets to be changed or taped over frequently. I like firing from around 3 1/2 yards at 3 inch circles that have been printed, drawn, or spray painted on the target. (This scales to a 6 inch circle at 7 yards.) As simple as this may seem, this type of target allows you to practice a wide variety of shooting and gun-handling tasks: the draw stroke, ready positions, multiple shots on one target, transitions between targets, one-handed aimed fire, reloads, and simulated malfunction clearances come immediately to mind. The goal is to keep all shots on the dots.

Ron Avery's "trigger bar" target, consisting of three rectangular boxes on an 8 1/2 x 11 inch piece of paper, can

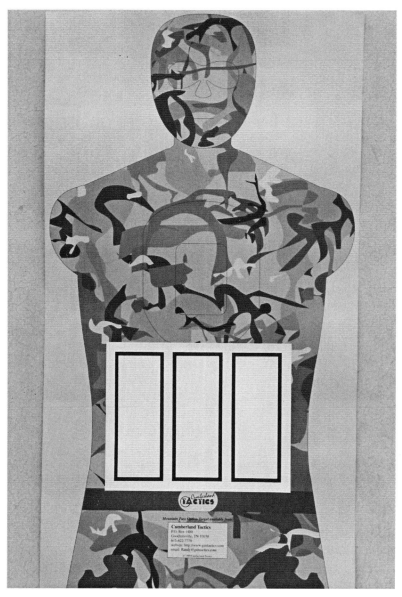

A Ron Avery "trigger bar" target shown with the Cumberland Tactics Mountain Pass Option silhouette. (Andy Stanford)

help you to reduce your split times, i.e., interval between shots. (You can easily make these on your home computer, but please print "The Practical Shooting Academy" on them so Ron gets due credit for the idea.) At a distance of 3 1/2 yards, fire six rounds at the first box at one shot per second. Then shoot a separate string of six at the middle box at a half second per shot. Lastly, engage the final box as fast as you think you can keep them in the rectangle, but a bit beyond your comfort zone. At one second per shot you should be able to consciously reset the trigger after weapon discharge. At a half second your reset will have to occur as the gun is in recoil. At maximum speed, you will not hit consistently without a correct grip and stance, the ability to see the sights throughout, and a reflexive reset-prep in time with the recoil.

Avery's target is excellent training for the "Bill Drill," developed by Bill Wilson. Draw and fire six rounds at a silhouette target from 7 yards. The string does not count unless every round hits the "A" zone. An IPSC Grandmaster can do this consistently in two seconds or less. With street gear, three seconds is quite fast. The Bill Drill is good for developing your ability to see more quickly.

As an overall evaluation of combat handgun skills on a single target, I like John Farnam's basic test. Stand 7 yards from a silhouette target with your gun loaded with six live rounds and one dummy. The dummy should not be the round in the chamber nor the last round in the magazine. Fire six body shots, clearing the dummy with a "tap-rack" when it comes up. Then reload from slide lock and fire two head shots. Move when not firing and during all weapon manipulations. Communicate with the ersatz assailant before the drill ("Stop!"), when drawing ("No!"), and when reloading ("Drop the weapon!" or "Back off!"), and practice talking with witnesses and responding authorities after the drill. Police and military personnel can substitute appropriate words and phrases for their particular applications.

Zero misses and at least 50 percent hits in the vital zone is a good minimum standard. An accomplished shooter should be able to keep 90 percent of his hits in the vital zone. Farnam requires 100 percent in an IPSC "A" zone or equivalent, but I feel this excessively slows down everyone except master level shooters. A rough guide for acceptable times is as follows:

- Start signal to first round: 2.5 seconds beginner, 2.0 intermediate, 1.5 expert, and 1.25 master.
- Split times between body shots: 1.0 beginner, 0.5 intermediate, 0.35 expert, and under 0.25 master. For head shot splits, add 0.25 to listed body splits; for beginners add 0.50.
- Malfunction clearance: subtract 0.5 from above draw times.
- Reload: add .75 second to above draw times; for beginner add 1.25.

I also shoot Farnam's drill from 4 yards with my dominant hand unsupported before the reload, then nondominant hand unsupported for the head shots. Given the likelihood of using one hand unsupported in the real world, it makes sense to conduct up to half of your practice firing one handed, particularly with the dominant side. Likewise, put in plenty of practice at contact-distance shooting using the previously described technique. And don't neglect kneeling, prone, and unorthodox firing positions. Use of cover usually requires something other than a textbook standing isosceles.

For multiple target practice, the Dozier drill is as good as any. Generally shot on five steel "pepper popper" targets, this exercise simulates a response to the multiple terrorists that kidnapped a NATO general in Italy. Space the targets at random intervals, at ranges from 5 to 10 yards, and paint them regularly to make sure you are getting surgical hits.

Speaking of targets, you must train to aim at the correct location on a human adversary. Many silhouettes feature "A" zones that are too large and centered too low, the standard IPSC and IDPA targets among them. Likewise the Gunsite, Front Sight, and ASAA (Chuck Taylor) targets are overly generous. The Mountain Pass Option target from Randy Cain is the most anatomically correct silhouette target I've found to date. On any humanoid target, hold yourself to the standard of fist-sized groups in the correct location at speed.

As you practice, work on one variable at a time. For example, concentrate on seeing the sight throughout the recoil cycle. Or focus on trigger reset and prep. You don't have to fire 500 rounds at a session; one or two boxes of ammo, used intelligently, can be plenty. Keep a log of the strings you fire in practice, and keep track of your progress. Don't dwell on poor shots or strings of fire; you can't change the past. Congratulate yourself for the good ones instead.

IDPA and IPSC/USPSA competition can be a useful adjunct to your practice sessions provided you don't develop bad tactical habits as a result. Avoid doing anything in a match that would be detrimental in an actual fight. Step off the attack line as you present your weapon, use cover wisely, vary the number of rounds fired on each target, and perform tactical post shooting procedures (i.e., assess, scan, and tac load, moving as appropriate and allowed) after each string, even if this is detrimental to your score sheet performance. Those motivated by a desire to improve their gunfighting skills, as opposed to a quest for trophies, must be willing to bleed ego on the match results to avoid shedding real blood in combat.

Lastly, if you have the wherewithal, I strongly recommend training with as many different world class instructors as possible. This includes those who teach the Weaver stance. These folks have much to offer in the realm of gun handling, tactics, and mind-set, even if their two-handed shooting technique is obsolescent. No one person has all the answers no matter what he or she may claim, and ultimately you must make up your own mind about what works best for you.